M000190835

GHOSTS WITHIN

GHOSTS WITHIN

Journeying Through PTSD

GARRY LEECH

Roseway Publishing
an imprint of Fernwood Publishing
HALIFAX & WINNIPEG

For my son Morgan

Copyright © 2019 Garry Leech

All rights reserved. No part of this book may be reproduced or transmitted
in any form by any means without permission in writing from the publisher,
except by a reviewer, who may quote brief passages in a review.

Editing: Brenda Conroy
Design: Tania Craan
Printed and bound in Canada

Published by Roseway Publishing
an imprint of Fernwood Publishing
32 Oceanvista Lane, Black Point, Nova Scotia, B0J 1B0
and 748 Broadway Avenue, Winnipeg, Manitoba, R3G 0X3
www.fernwoodpublishing.ca/roseway

Fernwood Publishing Company Limited gratefully acknowledges the financial
support of the Government of Canada through the Canada Book Fund,
the Canada Council for the Arts, the Province of Nova Scotia
and the Province of Manitoba for our publishing program.

Library and Archives Canada Cataloguing in Publication

Title: Ghosts within : journeying through PTSD / Garry Leech.
Names: Leech, Garry M., author.
Identifiers: Canadiana (print) 20190047836 | Canadiana (ebook) 20190047879
| ISBN 9781773632063
(softcover) | ISBN 9781773632070 (EPUB) | ISBN 9781773632087 (Kindle)
Subjects: LCSH: Leech, Garry M. | LCSH: Post-traumatic stress disorder—
Patients—Canada—Biography. |
LCSH: Journalists—Canada—Biography. | LCGFT: Autobiographies.
Classification: LCC RC552.P67 L44 2019 | DDC 616.85/210092—dc23

CONTENTS

PREFACE

A DECADE AGO I wrote a book titled *Beyond Bogotá: Diary of a Drug War Journalist in Colombia.* It was a memoir of the investigative journalism I'd conducted in Colombia's rural conflict zones over the previous eight years. But the story didn't end there. I continued to work as a war correspondent in Colombia for five more years and then returned on several occasions after that to teach a course on media and conflict at Javeriana University. Unfortunately for me and my family, what happened in Colombia didn't stay in Colombia. I brought the trauma I experienced and witnessed in that country's conflict zones home with me.

In 2016, I was diagnosed with post-traumatic stress disorder (PTSD), after exhibiting symptoms of the illness for the previous four years. My mental illness turned my world and that of my family upside down. This book tells the story of how my family and I have learned to live with this disorder. It describes in detail the horror that life becomes when someone who has experienced war or other violence brings their trauma home. While this book is in many ways a sequel to *Beyond Bogotá,* it is also a stand-alone work.

1

I have tried to tell my story as honestly as I can in order to provide the reader with valuable insights into what it is like to live with PTSD. I also place my story in the broader context of PTSD in our society. I have discovered that many people are uncomfortable around those who have a mental illness. While they don't hesitate to ask people with serious physical illnesses how they are doing and offer them support, many don't know how to respond to those afflicted with mental illness. I hope this book helps dissolve some of the stigma and fear so prevalent in attitudes towards people with PTSD and mental illness in general.

It is also my hope that others who suffer from this mental illness might read this book and feel affirmed and not so alone, because the feeling of isolation, that nobody understands what you are going through, is one of the worst aspects of PTSD. Additionally, I hope that my story provides some insights and comfort to the loved ones of those who endure PTSD, so that they may better understand what their family member or friend is experiencing.

It is estimated that eight million people in the United States and more than three million Canadians have PTSD, leading some to argue that the mental illness exists in near epidemic proportions, particularly since the wars in Iraq and Afghanistan. But these numbers are likely low because the illness often goes undiagnosed and untreated. In many ways, it is an invisible epidemic that mostly impacts individuals and families behind closed doors. However, it is not only those like me who have experienced war that are enduring this mental illness. In fact, the largest demographic in North America with PTSD is women who have suffered rape or sexual abuse. And the women with PTSD I've talked with have told me that, even though their traumatic experiences were very different to mine, their resulting mental illness often manifests itself in strikingly similar ways.

For those readers with PTSD who are concerned that they might be triggered by graphic accounts of the traumatic events depicted in this book, nearly all the descriptions of my traumatic experiences are represented in the form of intrusive memories: they are easily identifiable because they are in gray-shaded boxes separated from the main body of text throughout the book. However, there are also several brief descriptions of traumatic experiences that appear in the main body of the text.

I describe witnessing a rape on page 107 and provide an account of being held captive at gunpoint on page 120. I feel that these two experiences need to be included in the main body of the text in order to contextualize the therapy I was engaged in at the time. There are also several brief accounts of the traumatic experiences of Colombians I've encountered who likely have PTSD and these appear on pages 62–65. I feel it is necessary to include these to highlight how widespread trauma is for those who have no choice but to live their lives immersed in war. I'm providing the page numbers to these various descriptions of trauma so those who wish to skip them can do so.

I would not be here today to tell my story if it were not for some incredible and compassionate people. First and foremost, I will be forever in the debt of my partner, Terry, for being by my side through the darkest moments. She has exhibited a level of compassion that is almost incomprehensible to me. I want to sincerely thank my sons, Morgan and Owen, who have also been there for me day in and day out, comforting me and lifting my spirits with their positive energy—and giving me a reason to live. Additionally, I owe a huge debt of gratitude to my therapists, Todd Vassallo and Emily Bushell; Todd for bringing me back from the edge and Emily for giving me back my life.

I also wish to acknowledge the friends of Morgan and Owen, who, along with my sons, repeatedly filled my world with the uplifting energy that only children can generate. The sound of children playing was one of the only things that gave me any sense of joy during my darkest times, and for that I thank my grandchildren, Kathleen and Dylan, as well as Sadie, Olivia, Leon, Jade and Mady.

My gratitude also goes out to those big kids who have been there for me in various ways throughout this ordeal: my family Johan Gallardo, Karyn Leech Frazeur, Donald Leech, Norma Leech, Michele Villaneuve; and friends Amber Buchanan, Joanne Citrigno, Carolyn Claire, Stephen Harris, Tracey Harris, Evelyn Jones, Stephen Law, Barbara Miller, Wayne Miller and Stephen Paul. My thanks go to those who read early drafts of the manuscript and provided valuable feedback: Janet Bickerton, Amber Buchanan, Emily Bushell, Aviva Chomsky, Nicky Duenkel, Terry Gibbs, Tracey Harris, Stephen Law, Barbara Miller, Stephen Paul, Judy Pratt and Todd Vassallo. Finally, I thank the Roseway Publishing team: Beverley Rach, Errol Sharpe, Brenda Conroy, Debbie Mathers, Tania Craan and Curran Faris.

CHAPTER 1

THE BREAKDOWN

THE IMAGES KEPT INVADING my mind. A faceless massacre victim. A woman being raped. A guerrilla fighter holding a gun to my head. A legless landmine casualty. A body hacked open with a machete. The images wouldn't go away. I couldn't stop myself from thinking about them. The ghosts of my past were coming back to haunt me. It felt like they lived inside me and that they now controlled me. And along with the images came a flood of emotions—anger, sadness, guilt, remorse, self-hatred and helplessness—besieging me from all angles.

My mind felt like it was exploding. It was like an avalanche, as the different emotions collided with each other inside my head, crashing down and flooding over me, wave after wave. It was overwhelming. I just wanted it to stop. I sat in the chair in the corner of my bedroom drinking a bottle of El Dorado rum. But the alcohol wasn't numbing me; it wasn't stopping me from spiraling down.

I continued to sit there with my head in my hands, overwhelmed by the images and conflicting emotions. I began banging the palms of my hands against my head.

"Make it go away," I pleaded in desperation to no one.

The episode intensified over the next couple of hours until it reached the point that I felt the only way to end it, the only escape, was to kill myself. I imagined ways to do it. I didn't have a gun in the house, so that wasn't an option. I also didn't have medication to overdose on. I did have a Stanley knife in my toolbox in the cupboard above the washing machine. I went and retrieved the knife, returned to the bedroom and placed it on the dresser beside me. I sat there staring at the knife. I imagined holding it in my hand and sliding out the razor-sharp blade. I then envisioned sticking that blade into my wrist and slowly cutting along the artery that runs up the forearm, visualizing the blood pouring out of the cut. I thought about how liberating it would be to die.

But in that moment, as in all the other moments that I'd contemplated suicide, my thoughts went to my sons, Morgan and Owen. How could I do such a terrible thing to them when they were so young? It was agonizing to think of what losing their father might do to them. It would be the cruelest act. The thought of killing myself eventually passed. Once again, I'd been saved by Morgan and Owen.

While the thought of committing suicide passed, the emotional pain crashing around inside my head didn't. I got out of the chair and began pacing around the small room, pleading for the thoughts, feelings and images to go away. I then began punching myself in the face.

"It's never going to stop," I yelled angrily while hitting myself.

And it didn't stop. I began banging my head hard against the wall. Eventually, slowly, the emotional pain did begin to subside. I seemed to be regaining control. As the episode wound down I felt utterly exhausted and emotionally drained. I also felt simultaneously relieved and filled with dread, because I knew that I would have to endure another episode the following day or the one after that. For months, those episodes occurred every few days; they were relentless.

> I looked down at the body of a short woman dressed in a dark blue tee-shirt. She had a bullet hole in her cheek. It was a small round hole in the midst of dark purple bruises and dried blood. Most disturbing, however, was her rounded belly pushing out against the dirty blue shirt—she was clearly in an advanced stage of pregnancy.

Those episodes began after I had an emotional breakdown in the city of Cali in Colombia in November 2016. I was sitting by myself in a bar one evening enjoying a pint of local microbrewed beer. The place was decorated to look like an old Irish pub, but the wood paneling was far too new and fake-looking to be convincing. I sat alone at the bar as Latin music videos played on a flat-screen television mounted on the wall amidst shelves stocked with bottles of rum, whiskey and aguardiente. Two of the small tables situated against the wall behind me were occupied by trendy young couples happily experiencing a Latin American version of European culture.

While sitting there musing about my surroundings, I suddenly burst into tears. The tears came out of nowhere and just flooded down my cheeks. I couldn't stop them. I didn't know why I was bawling, but I was conscious of being in a public place. The dark-haired, middle-aged female bartender, dressed in conventional white shirt and black vest bartender attire, glanced in my direction but said nothing. Feeling self-conscious about my sudden and inexplicable public display of emotion, I quickly paid my tab and got out of there. I flagged down a taxi and headed back to my hotel. I was soon safely ensconced in my room, where the tears continued to flow. I had never been one for crying, so I was more than a little taken aback by this sudden outburst.

I was in Cali to teach a course on media and conflict as part of a master's program in human rights at Javeriana University. The city of Cali sat nestled in a valley between two ranges of the Andes Mountains. The city had a southern California feel to it—sprawling and laid back. I'd been invited to teach the course because of my work as a war correspondent covering Colombia's armed conflict. It was an intensive course that ran eight hours a day for three days, and I was teaching it for the third time in twelve months when my breakdown occurred.

Three days prior to my meltdown in the bar, I'd been speaking to two Colombian human rights workers about the deaths from malnutrition of more than four thousand Indigenous children in northern Colombia. It was a region I'd worked in on numerous occasions investigating the human rights and environmental consequences of Latin America's largest open-pit coalmine, which supplied coal to power plants in the United States, Europe and Canada, including my home province of Nova Scotia. The foreign-owned Cerrejón Mine was a contributor to the children's deaths because it used most of the region's water, thereby leaving an insufficient amount for local farmers to cultivate the crops they depended on for food.

The day after that conversation, one of my female students took me aside and, as tears welled in her eyes, she pleaded with me to go to the Colombian Amazon to investigate armed groups who were forcing Indigenous children into prostitution in that part of the country. It was a region I had worked in only a few years earlier where I'd discovered that a Canadian mining company was exploring the possibility of extracting coltan, a rare metal situated on Indigenous lands.

Most of my students were Colombian human rights defenders and NGO workers and, on the previous two occasions that I'd taught the course, several had asked me to visit their communities to investigate various issues. But I hadn't conducted investigative journalism in Colombia's rural conflict zones since 2012. That year, I began homeschooling my eldest son, Owen, which required me cutting back on my journalism work. So, while I still viewed myself as an investigative journalist, I'd politely declined their requests because I simply did not have the time due to my commitments to home schooling and part-time university teaching.

However, that latest appeal to investigate Indigenous child prostitution elicited a different response in me. As usual, I stated verbally that I doubted I would be able to travel to the region because of time constraints. But inside, I experienced a new and disturbing reaction. While talking with her, I suddenly realized that I didn't *want* to investigate that human rights crisis. The thought of returning to a conflict zone filled me with anxiety. For the first time, I wasn't declining an invitation to investigate a story because of time and logistical reasons, but because I couldn't handle the stress of working in a war zone again. This response shocked me.

My work in Colombia's remote conflict zones meant that I often stayed in primitive lodgings and ate whatever food was available. But while teaching the course in Cali, I resided in a luxurious, four-star hotel and dined in gourmet restaurants, courtesy of the private university that had hired me. I could not reconcile the luxurious working and living conditions I was enjoying with the feeling that I should be in the countryside investigating Indigenous children dying from malnutrition or being forced into prostitution. But I didn't want to have to deal with the stress of working in conflict zones again. I didn't feel that I could cope with it. I *wanted* to be in that luxury hotel. And that led to me being consumed with guilt and anger—both at myself and at a world I perceived to be full of injustice.

> The silence inside the jeep was suddenly broken when, directly behind my head, I heard the distinctive metallic sound of a slide on a gun being pulled back to shift a bullet into the chamber. I froze. For a terrifying second, I held my breath and waited for the crack of a gunshot. It didn't come, and I slowly exhaled. Then the thought crossed my mind that the guerrillas might be taking me into the jungle to execute me.

I sat in an armchair in my Cali hotel room reflecting on the path that had led me to this point in my life. My interest in Latin America had been initiated by a posting to Panama when I was in the US Marines. It had been further piqued by subsequent visits to Latin America as a civilian, which included my first encounter with war. During the 1980s, the US-backed military in El Salvador was fighting against a leftist insurgency. I was caught up in this conflict when I was detained and imprisoned for eight days by the Salvadoran military.

During that imprisonment I witnessed brutal abuses, including the gang rape of my female cellmate and the beating of male prisoners. Further disturbing was the fact that those horrors were perpetrated by soldiers who were being funded with my tax dollars. While I had been born and raised in England, I had lived in the United States since I was fifteen. And the government of my new home was supporting the military responsible for my detention and the abuses I witnessed. It was this and subsequent experiences in Latin America that led me to return to university and become an investigative journalist whose work was rooted in the global struggle for social justice.

Colombia was the first foreign country I worked in as a journalist. I had previously visited the South American nation in 1989, but my initial experience there as a reporter occurred in 2000. For the next thirteen years I spent a couple of months annually investigating the US military intervention and human rights issues in the country's rural conflict zones. I also worked in other countries, including Venezuela, Cuba and Palestine (West Bank), but my primary focus was Colombia.

I had witnessed horrific injustices in Colombia's conflict zones. I'd visited massacre sites, and the images of those dead bodies would remain ingrained in my memory. I had seen peasants who'd lost limbs to landmines and sick children who'd been poisoned by chemicals sprayed on them by anti-drug fumigation planes. There were the villagers whose community had been occupied by right-wing paramilitaries, who systematically raped most of the women and girls. There was the woman who spent a long night lying wounded with her baby amidst the dead bodies of 119 women and children in the rubble of a church bombed by leftist guerrillas. And there were the countless women and children who'd been forcibly displaced from their homes and lands and who had to live the precarious lives of refugees in dangerous shantytowns.

It was not only violence and terror perpetrated against others that I was exposed to, but also the threat of violence against me. Working in conflict zones required functioning constantly with a heightened sense of awareness. I was on edge all the time, anticipating a sudden burst of gunfire, a bomb attack or an encounter with a military checkpoint. On numerous occasions I'd accompanied army, guerrilla and paramilitary patrols in constant anticipation of being ambushed or stepping on a landmine. On one occasion, I was surrounded by automatic gunfire in the middle of a major nighttime street battle that occurred when guerrillas attacked the town I was working in.

I regularly came upon the checkpoints of armed groups never knowing whether I was going to be detained and inter-rogated—or kidnapped or killed. On three occasions I'd been detained and held captive by armed groups. During two of those detentions I was held on remote farms in the jungle and interrogated and threatened with death. They were the most terrifying experiences of my life. The sense of impotence was overwhelming. I had no control over whether I would walk out of there alive. My future—if I were to have one—rested entirely on the decisions of local military commanders. Even at home I wasn't safe from the threat of violence because I received death threats via email.

As I sat in my hotel room reflecting on those experiences, I couldn't help but think about how much I hated war. While growing up, history classes in school had been full of stories of war. In fact, the timeline of our history seemed to be marked by wars, one after another. War was usually portrayed as one group of uniformed soldiers fighting against another group of uniformed soldiers. War was even portrayed as heroic, full of glory. But there was nothing heroic in war; there was no glory. I knew this from seeing war and its impacts with my own eyes.

It was not only the armed combatants who bore the brunt of war; it was also the civilian population. In war, it was unarmed men, women and children who were the principal victims of the violence. They suffered virtually unimaginable horrors. War revealed the darkest depths of human depravity. That reality was not taught in history classes. And after spend-ing so many years witnessing the worst of what human beings were capable of doing to each other, it was difficult for me to have faith in humanity any longer. It was difficult for me to believe that human beings could create a better world, a more humane world.

It might seem obvious to most people that repeatedly witnessing massacre sites and being detained and held at gunpoint by armed groups are traumatic experiences, but those and many other encounters had become so routine for me that they felt normal. Such experiences simply came with the territory, and I didn't stop to consider how they might be negatively affecting me. I felt that I had some special skillset that allowed me to do this type of work and to cope with the horrific things I witnessed and experienced. In fact, I felt that I could handle anything.

Obviously, I was wrong, because on my last evening in Cali, after several days of deep reflection and rumination on war and my role as a journalist, I had the breakdown in the bar. The realization that I no longer wanted to be a war correspondent seemed to open up my subconscious mind, releasing all the trauma-related emotions buried deep inside me, emotions that had been hidden away to allow me to be able to continue functioning in conflict zones. And so, the flood gates opened, and those emotions finally came pouring out—and I cried and cried and cried.

The victims were three men who appeared to be in their twenties. Two of the bodies were lying on the white tile floor, one without a shirt. They both had bullet holes in their foreheads. I stared down at the shirtless corpse, whose eyes were open and staring blankly into space. A pool of blood was forming on the floor underneath his head, leaking from the exit wound in the rear of his skull. The third victim lay on the opposite side of the room. His torso had been slashed open, most likely with a machete.

When I arrived home from Cali, the emotional turmoil continued, and my partner, Terry, convinced me to see a therapist because she thought I might have post-traumatic stress disorder (PTSD). I pulled into the small parking lot in front of the century-old house in which the therapist's office was located, nervous about the impending encounter. I was not familiar with therapy. I also was not comfortable displaying my emotions in front of men. And I still could not stop crying, even though it had been a week since my breakdown. I entered the office full of trepidation, and my worst fears were realized when I spent the entire one-hour session bawling. But, surprisingly, I didn't feel as uncomfortable as I thought I would crying in front of a man I didn't know. I was probably beyond caring at that point.

Todd Vassallo was a middle-aged man of average build with short gray hair and a calming presence. He had specialized in treating PTSD for many years. Todd began our session by explaining that with PTSD the traumatic experiences occurred in the past but the symptoms, or emotional responses, continued in the present. He said I should try to focus on the present moment in that room and recognize that nothing bad was happening.

I scanned the room. It was large enough to comfortably accomodate an average-sized desk and two armchairs without feeling crowded. The walls had been recently painted a pastel green colour, but the old rustic windows betrayed the age of the building. Todd was seated in a well-worn, black, imitation-leather armchair while I was slouched in an identical chair directly opposite him. As I looked around the room my eyes locked on a floor lamp standing beside Todd's chair. My thoughts immediately went to the Indigenous children dying from malnutrition in Colombia so that we could have electricity. As I sat there with tears streaming down my cheeks, I wasn't just sad, I was also angry.

"The things I've seen didn't only occur in the past, they're still going on now," I angrily explained. And, pointing to the lamp, I stated, "Every time we turn on a light we contribute to the killing of children in Colombia."

"But those deaths are not happening in this room at this moment," Todd calmly said.

We went back and forth. I couldn't focus solely on what was happening in that room without making the connections to broader issues that resulted in human suffering. After all, that had been the point of my journalism for the previous two decades. And one thing my journalism work had made evident to me was that our lifestyles in rich countries like Canada and the United States were intimately linked to the misery endured by millions in poor nations. The burning of Colombian coal so that we could have electricity was just the most convenient example for me to throw at Todd, because it was still fresh in my mind following the conversation I'd had with the Colombian human rights workers only ten days earlier. In that moment, that lamp constituted the umbilical cord that kept me connected to Colombia.

Todd tried to get me to understand that my anger in and of itself wasn't helping either the Indigenous children in Colombia or me. This might seem obvious to a rational person. But I was not a rational person at that moment. Far from it. And that is part of what was so terrifying. I had always been a sensible and logical human being, but now I was an emotional wreck seething with anger and sadness. To de-link my current personal predicament from the broader analysis of global politics would not only undermine my integrity as a journalist, it would undermine my integrity as a person. In my mind, it meant I would no longer be the person I thought I was.

Todd understood what I was saying and feeling, but his primary concern at that moment was to help me get to a place where I could at least function without falling apart. And then, once there, I could begin concerning myself again with how to use my privilege as a white male living in a rich country to help others, such as the Indigenous children in Colombia. He didn't succeed on that first visit, and I walked out of his office unconvinced. I drove home tearfully, wondering how therapy, or anything else for that matter, was going to help me.

CHAPTER 2

THE MEETING

I FIRST MET TERRY at a meeting in New York in the fall of 2002. She was the director of the North American Congress on Latin America (NACLA), and we were part of a diverse group of people organizing a conference on US foreign policy in Latin America. After the meeting, some of us went out for food and drinks, and Terry and I ended up engaged in a long conversation that revealed incredible similarities in our life trajectories.

We sat opposite each other drinking beers in the garden patio of an East Village restaurant. The garden was surrounded by a tall wooden fence on three sides and the rear entrance to the restaurant on the fourth. A large oak tree towered above us with its branches and leaves spreading out over the patio like a giant umbrella.

I explained to Terry that I was born in Coventry, England. At the age of fifteen, my father's job as an engineer for multinational tractor manufacturer Massey Ferguson caused the family to move to the United States. We left the middle-class suburbs of industrial Manchester and settled into the middle-class suburbs of industrial Detroit. I wasn't happy following the move. In fact, I felt like a misfit in my new high school, an outsider who spoke and dressed strangely. I fled Detroit shortly after graduating high school at the age of eighteen and headed west to Los Angeles. Six months later, seeking new adventures, I joined the US Marines and was deployed to Panama.

My military activities in Panama mostly consisted of hours upon tedious hours of guarding US naval installations along the Panama Canal. It also involved many other mind-numbing, time-filling chores that were primarily designed to keep us busy and out of trouble. I quickly grew to detest the dehumanizing, desensitizing and tedious nature of military life and responded to it by becoming increasingly disobedient of my superiors. When a thirty-five-day stint in the brig failed to curb my insubordination, the commanding officer of the Marine detachment in Panama offered me a general discharge, which I gladly accepted.

During the decade following my discharge from the Marines, I returned to Latin America on a couple of occasions—one of which involved my detention in El Salvador—and lived in a variety of locales across the United States while working an assortment of jobs. I was a construction worker in Houston. A blues concert promoter in Iowa City. A security guard in Detroit. A butcher in nearby Ann Arbor. I also learned how to play guitar and began writing songs. At twenty-nine, I moved to New York City to focus on a music career, driving a taxi to support myself while performing in several bands. While attending a New Year's Eve party in 1992, I met and later married a native New Yorker named Jacqui. But by the mid-1990s I was becoming increasingly disenchanted with the music scene and more and more interested in US foreign policy in Latin America following further visits to the region. So I returned to university and, after graduation, began working as a journalist.

As we sat in that garden patio drinking our umpteenth beer,

I learned that Terry was seven years younger than me and was born in Ontario, Canada, to British parents. She spent half of her childhood in Canada and the other half growing up in Wales, where her parents owned a pub. While the roots of my political awakening lay in my early experiences in Latin America, Terry's lay in the five months she spent living in rural Malawi in Africa as part of a Canada World Youth program when she was twenty-one years old. On her return from Africa she found herself drawn to political activism, having been affected by the poverty and oppression she'd witnessed in Malawi.

Terry earned her PhD with a dissertation focused on El Salvador and Nicaragua, where she'd lived and worked for a year and a half during the mid-1990s. She then worked in academia briefly before teaching English for three months in Palestinian refugee camps in Beirut, Lebanon. Upon returning to North America, she had taken the job at NACLA, a mere three weeks before our encounter.

As we sat there talking and drinking I was mesmerized by Terry's account of her life and the similarities to my own. We had both been raised apolitically in the Anglo-dominated cultures of Britain and North America. We had both become politically engaged as a result of personal experiences in poor nations of the global South. And we'd both travelled and worked extensively in difficult conditions in Latin America and had developed a passion for the region. Additionally, Terry was a tall, beautiful, single woman with long wavy brown hair and a radiant air I found captivating. I, on the other hand, was married. Nevertheless, I went home that evening intrigued by Terry.

Shortly after that first meeting, Terry invited me to speak on a panel that NACLA was hosting at the World Social Forum in Porto Alegre, Brazil, in January 2003. The forum was a gathering of tens of thousands of social activists from around the world exchanging ideas and strategizing ways to create a more humane world. After our panel discussion on race issues in Latin America, Terry and I went out for drinks. And so began one of the most magical nights of my life.

We sat at the bar in a small establishment just down the street from Terry's hotel, talking all night about our personal lives and our work in great detail. I couldn't believe that I was having such an intimate conversation with someone who in one way was almost a stranger, and yet in another felt like my oldest friend. We connected in an intense and powerful way, both emotionally and intellectually. It was an incredibly passionate night, even though kissing represented the only physical contact. Our conversation finally concluded at six o'clock in the morning because I had to leave for the airport to catch a flight to Colombia.

We walked out of the bar onto the empty street. The sun was beginning to emerge from behind the rooftops as we kissed each other goodbye. Terry began walking one way to her hotel and I went in the opposite direction in search of a taxi. As I was walking away I heard Terry's voice call out my name. I turned and saw her standing in the middle of the deserted street.

"What's going to happen when we get back to New York?" she asked.

In my best Humphrey Bogart impersonation, I replied, "I don't know. But we'll always have Porto Alegre." I saw her smile and, as I turned and walked away, I knew that I was in love with her.

I heard the woman's muffled cries and men's laughter from behind that closed door, leaving little doubt about what was taking place. I felt so helpless sitting there with my thumbs tied together behind my back while they raped that defenceless woman. I thought of shouting for help, but realized it might only result in more soldiers joining in on the abuse.

When I arrived in Colombia I couldn't stop thinking about Terry. But even though I was in love with her, I couldn't imagine walking away from my ten-year relationship with Jacqui. Despite the troubles Jacqui and I had been experiencing over the previous couple of years, it had largely been a good ten years. Jacqui worked as the manager of a small non-profit organization that published a monthly political newsletter. She had been supportive of my desire to return to university and become a journalist, but after a while I began to feel suffocated in our relationship. Jacqui's understandable concern for my safety in Colombia's war zones resulted in her trying to dissuade me from working in the most violent regions of the country and from investigating some of the more dangerous issues. But I felt compelled to go wherever the story took me.

I felt I wasn't getting the sort of emotional support I needed. But that wasn't Jacqui's fault; after all, she had no way of relating to my work, or perhaps I never really gave her the opportunity to be there for me. Regardless of the reasons, we were growing apart, and neither of us was particularly happy with our marriage. But I had always believed that one way or another we would work through our problems, and I had never seriously considered ending our relationship—until I met Terry.

While working in Colombia on that visit, I constantly went back and forth regarding what I should do when I returned to New York. One minute I'd decide that I should leave Jacqui; the next I would decide to tell Terry there was no way that we could have a relationship. And then, one evening, I found myself caught in the middle of a prolonged street battle when guerrillas attacked the town I was working in. Afterwards, I was not only relieved to have survived the battle, but also surprised to discover that a great part of that relief was due to the thought of being able to see Terry again.

Telling Jacqui that I had met someone else was one of the most difficult things I'd ever had to do. Not so much because it was uncomfortable for me, though it was, but because I still loved her and didn't want to cause her pain. She asked me to leave immediately, so I threw some clothes into a bag and headed out the door. While part of me felt distressed about the end of my marriage, another part of me felt liberated.

I moved into Terry's small studio apartment in the Crown Heights section of Brooklyn. She went to work every day at NACLA, while I continued to write articles and travel back and forth to Colombia. We also attended conferences in Barcelona and Dallas, and worked together in Colombia that summer, investigating how the conflict was impacting Indigenous Peoples in the remote jungles of the Chocó region. During that trip to Colombia, we spent a romantic week together on vacation at a deserted beach on the country's Pacific Coast. The beach was deserted because guerrillas had kidnapped a group of tourists from that location several weeks earlier.

At the same time as our relationship was blossoming, Terry was becoming discontented with her work as an administrator of a non-profit organization. She wanted to return to academia. We had also endured the agonizing loss of a twin pregnancy at five months, which made a change in scenery even more appealing. And so, eighteen months into our relationship, we moved to beautiful Cape Breton Island in Nova Scotia, Canada. Terry had been offered a full-time position teaching international politics at Cape Breton University. I was unexpectedly offered a part-time teaching position, which was perfect because it allowed me to continue spending a couple of months a year working as a freelancer conducting investigative journalism in Colombia's rural conflict zones. I also began a seven-year stretch during which I wrote six books and became a Canadian citizen.

I also became a father. In 2006, our son Owen was born. I cannot describe the pure joy that I felt. Terry and I decided that we didn't want Owen to be an only child and so, two years later, our second son, Morgan, entered the world. Terry and I were ecstatic. Our life with two small children was nothing less than wonderful, and I went about my work both in Colombia and at home with my nuclear family constituting the centre of my universe. Little did I know that my family was about to suddenly increase in size again.

In December 2010, I discovered that I had a daughter in Panama. She had located me through the Internet, which was not difficult because of my journalism work. Her name was Johan and she was twenty-nine years old. Johan had a two-year-old daughter named Kathleen. I was a grandfather! Terry handled this new discovery with incredible understanding and compassion, unquestioningly accepting that Johan and Kathleen were going to be part of our family.

Two months after receiving that initial email, Terry and I flew to Panama. The morning after our arrival, we walked out of our hotel room and took the elevator down to the lobby. Waiting there were my daughter and granddaughter. Seeing Johan and Kathleen for the first time was a powerful emotional experience. As I stared at Johan, I recognized the same auburn hair that I'd had when I was younger, a colour that was rare in Panama. The nervousness I'd been feeling at the prospect of meeting my grownup daughter for the first time evaporated almost immediately when we hugged. Over the next week

Johan and I had long talks and began to get to know each other. Her mother had never married and had raised Johan and her brother single-handedly, working as a domestic servant for most of her life in order to survive in difficult economic circumstances.

The following year Terry and I took Morgan and Owen to Panama, and we spent a magical ten days with the whole family together. Johan has since had a second child, Dylan. Our newest Panamanian family members provided me with a more intimate connection with Latin America than I'd ever imagined possible. But while everything in my life appeared to be perfect, shifts were beginning to take place that would turn our world upside down.

Throughout most of my life I had not been a particularly depressed person. I had not exhibited much of a temper during my childhood or throughout my twenties. However, during the latter years of my marriage with Jacqui, I would lose my temper on occasion. It was not a common occurrence, but at times I would be angry enough to punch a wall or some other inanimate object. Those infrequent outbursts of anger persisted after Terry and I began living together. They were most often triggered by my frustrations with a malfunctioning computer, and Terry humorously labelled the person that appeared during those outbursts as Computer Monster, or CM for short. Thankfully, those flare-ups were brief and continued to be relatively infrequent until 2012.

That year Terry and I decided Owen should be home-schooled because of the problems he was having in the local school. He had difficulty sitting still in a chair for hours on end and, because he constantly appeared to be distracted, the teacher singled him out by making him sit front and centre every day. The teacher told us that Owen had difficulty focusing and as a result was struggling to learn to read and write. Owen was also being bullied by another student, and the school failed to effectively address that problem. So I took on the responsibility of homeschooling Owen (and, two years later, Morgan too). I quickly learned that while Owen did struggle to focus when forced to sit still for long periods, when allowed to move around, his capacity to concentrate and learn was immense. And by twelve years of age he was reading university-level texts.

My commitment to homeschooling meant that something in my work life had to give. Because my part-time teaching at the university constituted steady work and regular pay-cheques, I decided that my investigative journalism would have to be sacrificed. This meant that I would no longer travel to Colombia to conduct investigations in the country's conflict zones, although I would continue to write analysis and opinion pieces on global political issues from home. I believed this period of my life without investigative journalism would only be temporary and that I would return to the frontlines at some point in the future. It was following this shift that changes in my behaviour and personality began to occur, although Terry and I were not immediately aware that those changes were happening. We certainly had no idea that they were related to PTSD.

CHAPTER 3

THE UNRAVELLING

DESPITE MY SKEPTICISM FOLLOWING that first therapy session with Todd, I returned and saw him on a weekly basis. In my therapy and through my own research I learned that PTSD can be caused by a single traumatic event or, as in my case, an accumulation of traumas, which is known as complex PTSD. A traumatic event can be any number of things, including war, sexual assault, a traffic accident, a natural disaster or witnessing death. According to the *Diagnostic and Statistical Manual of Mental Disorders* (DSM-5), for an event to be classified as "traumatic" several diagnostic criteria must be met, including (1) exposure to actual or threatened death, serious injury or sexual violence; and (2) directly experiencing the event, witnessing it in person or being indirectly exposed to the event (i.e., repeatedly hearing or seeing details about the event).

In Canada, more than three million people will suffer from PTSD during their lifetime. Meanwhile, about eight million people in the United States suffer from the mental illness, and, contrary to popular belief—and contrary to what I believed— soldiers are not the most likely group to be afflicted. While up to 30 percent of soldiers in combat get PTSD, 40 percent of women who have been sexually assaulted suffer with the disorder. And unbeknownst to me during all my years of work in Colombia, 29 percent of war correspondents end up with PTSD.

The term post-traumatic stress disorder is relatively new, but the illness is not. Two thousand years ago, in his classic works *The Illiad* and *The Odyssey,* the ancient Greek author Homer described how war changed men and about the difficulties they faced upon returning home. In *The Odyssey,* Homer wrote about how, after Odysseus had returned from war, the "great Odysseus melted into tears, running down from his eyes to wet his cheeks ... trying to beat the day of doom from home and children." Similarly, four hundred years ago, William Shakespeare described the symptoms of PTSD in *Henry IV* when Lady Percy spoke to her husband Hotspur following his return from combat:

Why dost thou bend thine eyes upon the earth,
And start so often when thou sit'st alone?
Why hast thou lost the fresh blood in thy cheeks
And given my treasures and my rights of thee
To thick-eyed musing and curst melancholy?
In thy faint slumbers I by thee have watched,
And heard thee murmur tales of iron wars.

In the late 1800s, psychiatrists began diagnosing women who were emotionally disturbed as suffering from "hysteria." Sigmund Freud noted that many of those women had reported being sexually abused as children, thereby making the first link between sexual abuse and PTSD. During World War One, the focus returned to men in combat when the term "shell shock" was used to describe soldiers whose mental health was negatively affected by war. And in World War Two, the term "battle fatigue" was coined. It wasn't until after the Vietnam War that afflicted soldiers were said to be suffering from post-traumatic stress disorder, a term that was officially recognized by the American Psychiatric Association in 1980.

I discovered that PTSD is related to a change in the way the brain functions and can occur with various degrees of severity. Researchers using magnetoencephalography (MEG) scans have shown that the brains of people with PTSD have been physically transformed by trauma, unlike the brains of people who have experienced trauma but do not have the disorder. The brain is a complex system, but for the sake of examining PTSD we can refer to the triune brain model, which separates the brain into three parts. The first part is the rational brain, or prefrontal cortex. It is the part of the brain that controls impulses and allows us to analyze and think things through. The second part is the emotional brain, or limbic system, which contains the amygdala and hippocampus. The amygdala is responsible for our emotional responses, especially to potential threats, while the hippocampus processes and then files away those emotional experiences in the appropriate place in our memory bank. The final part is the reptilian brain, which triggers the fight, flight or freeze response when the amygdala signals that we are in danger.

During a traumatic experience, the amygdala identifies a threat and the reptilian brain immediately seizes control from the rational brain and shuts down all non-essential body and mind activities as it kicks into survival mode. A corresponding increase in stress hormones helps the body to fight, flee or freeze. Following the traumatic experience, when the threat has subsided, the reptilian brain relinquishes control back to the rational brain, and we return to the normal intellectual and problem-solving activities of daily life. Meanwhile, the hippocampus processes the emotional experience and integrates it into the mind's memory bank, where it takes its place alongside memories of other emotional experiences.

So, what does this look like in our daily life? Imagine you are walking along a path in the forest and suddenly see something in front of you that looks like a snake. Your response is to stop dead in your tracks. A second later, you realize that the object is just a stick. The amygdala initially recognized the stick as a threat (a snake) and the reptilian brain instantly seized control from the rational brain and put you in survival mode. You responded by immediately stopping; you froze. Only after you identified the object as a stick did the rational brain re-assume control, while the hippocampus processed the experience and filed it away in your memory bank as a false alarm.

There is no way that you could have prevented yourself from freezing when you thought you saw a snake because the reptilian brain reacts much faster than the rational brain. If that stick had actually been a snake and you'd had to wait for your rational brain to determine what the object was before you reacted, the snake might have bitten you. The reptilian brain's instant response has been essential for keeping humans alive in a dangerous world for millennia.

For those who have PTSD, the amygdala remains over-stimulated and fails to recognize that the threat has passed. Consequently, the reptilian brain doesn't return full control of the mind back to the rational brain, and the continuing production of stress hormones kills cells in the hippocampus. A person with PTSD has an overstimulated amygdala and under-active hippocampus, resulting in the mind and body failing to recognize that a threat has passed and preventing the brain from processing and filing the memory of a traumatic experience in its appropriate place. Consequently, the brain believes that the traumatic experience is still happening, and the mind and body remain in fight, flight or freeze mode.

Another time the amygdala perceives a threat is when someone startles us. Our heart immediately skips a beat and then begins to race. We might also respond by impulsively jumping backwards or even lashing out at the person. There is no way to prevent ourselves from being startled. The amygdala has perceived a threat and sent stress hormones surging through our body while the reptilian brain immediately assumes control and prepares us for fight, flight or freezing. When we realize that what startled us isn't a threat, the rational brain re-assumes control. The problem for people with PTSD is that the amygdala perceives almost every sound, person and place as a threat, so they live permanently in startle response mode.

Psychiatrist Bessel van der Kolk is medical director of the Trauma Center in the United States and one of the world's leading experts on PTSD. His book *The Body Keeps the Score* became my PTSD bible. Dr. van der Kolk points out that "trauma is much more than a story about something that happened long ago. The emotions and physical sensations that were imprinted during the trauma are experienced not as memories but as disruptive physical reactions in the present."

This short circuit in the brain means that the mind of a person with PTSD is stuck in a past traumatic event, which results in the person exhibiting "disruptive physical reactions in the present" in the form of the four types of symptoms of PTSD:

- re-experiencing (re-living the traumatic event);
- avoidance (avoiding reminders of the event);
- hyperarousal and hypervigilance (feeling on edge and on guard all the time); and
- negative changes in beliefs and feelings.

Re-experiencing occurs in the form of nightmares, flashbacks or intrusive memories that are triggered by certain situations, sights, sounds or smells and by conscious or subconscious thoughts of a traumatic experience. These triggers could include news reports, certain topics of conversation, specific noises or crowded places. Avoidance occurs when a person with PTSD tries to avoid situations that might trigger a re-experiencing. This often results in contraction, when a person shrinks their personal world down to a safe and manageable size, which often means not socializing much or rarely leaving home.

Hyperarousal is caused by an overstimulated amygdala constantly telling the reptilian brain that a threat is present when that is not the case. The person remains in a permanent state of hypervigilance and can be easily startled by sudden noises, feel uncomfortable in crowded places or have difficulty sleeping (insomnia). The constant state of hyperarousal and related anxiety can leave PTSD sufferers in a state of chronic fatigue. A negative change in beliefs and feelings also often occurs in people with PTSD because the perpetual fear they experience causes them to perceive the world as a dangerous place and leaves them with little faith that things can change for the better.

Because PTSD causes a person to repeatedly re-live past traumatic experiences, it is impossible for them to relax; the person is always in fear, on guard and expecting the worst. But these symptoms and their related behaviours are completely normal and appropriate in dangerous situations. That is why some combat veterans with PTSD, who feel completely dysfunctional when they return home, want to return to war, where their behaviour and the emotions they feel make sense. In a perverse irony, they feel safer when in danger.

Ultimately, PTSD is a mental illness that prevents a person from functioning as they normally would in a safe environment. Dr. van der Kolk explains:

We now know that trauma compromises the brain area that communicates the physical, embodied feeling of being alive. These changes explain why traumatized individuals become hypervigilant to threat at the expense of spontaneously engaging in their day-to-day lives. They also help us understand why traumatized people so often keep repeating the same problems and have such trouble learning from experience. We now know that their behaviors are not the result of moral failings or signs of lack of willpower or bad character—they are caused by actual changes in the brain.

Every so often one of the paramilitary fighters would interrogate me while awaiting word from their commander regarding what to do with the "gringo" journalist they had captured. In between those interrogations I waited silently while enduring almost unbearable fear and anxiety, which came and went in waves. I had seen firsthand in southern Colombia what the paramilitaries were capable of doing with machetes, chainsaws or any other instrument of death they might choose to use on me.

My therapy sessions with Todd and my research into PTSD helped Terry and me start to make sense of what had been happening to me over the four years leading up to my breakdown. Beginning in 2012, after I stopped working as a war correspondent, the most notable change had been an increase in the frequency of my angry outbursts. They were no longer only triggered by technology problems but by many other things too. Some innocuous comment by Terry could trigger an outburst. The boys making too much noise. The cat meowing. A Tupperware container without a lid could result in the offending object being thrown across the kitchen. An uncooperative window blind could find itself mangled. My forgetting to put out the recycling bags on pick-up day could trigger an angry outburst at myself. The most trivial of incidents would trigger disproportionate outbursts of anger.

As time passed, I felt more and more on edge. If Terry dropped a spoon on the kitchen floor when I was in the living room, it would feel as though my heart was jumping out of my chest and I would immediately feel intense anxiety in the pit of my stomach. My outward response would also be instantaneous.

"What the hell was that?" I would yell aggressively.

"It's just a spoon," Terry would answer.

"How hard is it to hold onto a spoon?" I would respond.

Unbeknownst to Terry and me at the time, I was existing in a state of hyperarousal. I was subconsciously switched on all the time. Because of my PTSD, my brain perceived everything, even the sound of a spoon hitting the floor, as a threat. This is a natural state of brain function in a war zone, where dangers are ever-present and therefore the amygdala is constantly on guard and ready to activate the reptilian brain to shift into survival mode. However, it is not a natural state of brain function when living in a safe environment. In fact, it is highly dysfunctional. But because of this state of hyperarousal, the sound of a spoon hitting the floor triggered a response in me equal to the reaction that would be triggered by the sound of a gunshot or an explosion in a war zone. So, while the actual threat had existed in the past, my emotional response occurred in the present. It was like living in a time warp.

Not surprisingly, Terry, Morgan and Owen often walked on eggshells around me, especially when they knew I was having a bad day. I was conscious of what was happening, even if I didn't yet understand why, and I began to feel guilty about what I was doing to Terry and the boys. But guilt only compounded the problem, because it made me get angry at myself. And anger, whether directed at myself or someone else, would suddenly appear out of nowhere. It was instantaneous. I could literally be sitting or talking calmly and suddenly *wham*! In a split second, I would be yelling or hitting something. Because the amygdala was constantly anticipating a threat, stress hormones were surging through my body. This boost in stress hormones gives a person the strength and adrenaline they need to either fight or flee when facing a threat. The problem for me was that those stress hormones were always present in my body, which left me in a permanent state of hyperarousal. I felt constantly on edge. It made me irritable and easily angered.

When someone did something to trigger me, I would have a two-fold response. Initially, I would be angry at them for whatever they did, which seemed like a healthy response to my malfunctioning reptilian brain at the time. But afterwards I would feel terribly guilty when my rational brain had reactivated and made evident that my response was a gross over-reaction. I would always apologize to Terry and the boys after an outburst. But how many times can a person keep apologizing while repeatedly engaging in the same problematic behaviour?

During those angry outbursts, Terry would attempt to calm me down, usually to no avail. My amygdala had activated my reptilian brain, which put me in survival mode. There would be no reasoning with me until my rational brain regained control. As the National Center for PTSD explains, "Anger is often a large part of a survivor's response to trauma. It is a core piece of the survival response in human beings. Anger helps us cope with life's stresses by giving us energy to keep going in the face of trouble or blocks. Yet anger can create major problems in the personal lives of those who have experienced trauma and those who suffer from PTSD."

Thankfully, my anger never manifested itself in physical attacks that targeted Terry or our sons. It only targeted inanimate objects. In fact, for the most part, Morgan and Owen had a calming effect on me despite the occasional bouts of irritability and anger that I directed towards them. Their upbeat and positive energy was one of the only things that could make me feel good, and the thought of doing harm to them was intolerable.

The presence of Morgan and Owen even helped me to have moments of feeling balanced and hopeful. That is why I could continue to homeschool them relatively effectively. I even liked it when their friends came over because the sound of children playing was such a joyous sound; it was such a celebration of life. For some reason, having kids around helped to ground me. Terry, on the other hand, was not so lucky. She bore the brunt of my dysfunctional behaviour. Thankfully, in those early years, such outbursts were still relatively sporadic, although they were slowly increasing in frequency.

We would later learn that Terry was experiencing secondary trauma due to living with someone with PTSD. Hyperarousal became a constant state for her too. Her hyperarousal was not PTSD-related, because it was not rooted in past traumatic experiences. Instead, it was rooted in the very real and present threat that I could react angrily at any moment. If she dropped something, she would freeze in anticipation of my response. If I was having a bad day, then she would be afraid that anything she said might set me off. Often, while driving home from work, Terry would worry about who she was going to encounter when she entered the house—Stalin or Santa, as she labelled my two personalities. Morgan and Owen also exhibited a similar level of hyperarousal.

During quieter moments before we knew I had PTSD, Terry would ask me, "Why can't you just pause for a moment before you explode and think about what's happening?" I would tell her that I just couldn't do it. The explosion would ignite so fast that I had no time to reflect. I could see the explosion happening, almost as though I were outside of my body watching myself. But I couldn't stop it. It didn't make sense to me—or to Terry. I had always been a person with a large degree of self-control who was disciplined and effective at managing or changing behaviours I didn't like. But now, I had no control over my reactions, and it felt like I had suddenly become possessed by an alien entity.

While Terry viewed me as either Santa or Stalin, I felt like Dr. Jekyll and Mr. Hyde. My normal rational and happy Dr. Jekyll personality would become the horrible Mr. Hyde in an instant. As the years went on, Mr. Hyde slowly took over and eventually became the dominant personality. I hated Mr. Hyde. But no matter how hard I tried, I could not get rid of him, or prevent him from rearing his ugly head. We didn't realize at the time that I couldn't prevent those outbursts because my amygdala was automatically activating my reptilian brain, which responded instantly, before my rational brain could analyze the situation. I was repeatedly seeing the snake and not the stick.

The military patrol I was accompanying consisted of two columns with each soldier maintaining a twenty-yard distance from the one ahead of him—thus ensuring that a single hand grenade wouldn't kill more than one of them. The atmosphere was tense and nerve-wracking, and I was constantly anticipating a sudden burst of gunfire or an explosion. Each time a soldier decided to investigate a vehicle, building or an individual, the entire patrol came to a halt. The soldiers and I would take cover behind trees or beside nearby buildings to guard against a possible rebel ambush.

During the years that this shift in my personality was occurring, my vigilance of my surroundings also began working in overdrive. This meant that I was constantly aware of every little thing that was going on around me. I would subconsciously register the precise location of everything in the house. I realized this was happening when I'd notice that an innocuous item, such as my iPod or the toaster, had been moved half an inch. I hadn't consciously memorized the location of those things, so I realized that I must have been subconsciously registering it, because I knew when any item in the house had been moved even a miniscule distance. My hypervigilance also caused me to scan every inch of my environment at all times, especially when I was outside the house. I was constantly on guard and needed to feel in control of every situation, because when I didn't feel in control, my mind began assuming that the worst was going to happen.

My view of the world was also shifting during those years; it was becoming increasingly negative. I had always been involved in campus activities and social justice activism. I was a member, and later director, of the Centre for International Studies at the university. Terry and I worked together to help organize the centre's annual social justice forum, which often brought in speakers that we had met through our work overseas. I enjoyed both my work with the centre and our constant engagement with students interested in social justice issues. I had also regularly attended the annual gathering of the Atlantic Regional Solidarity Network (ARSN) and participated in that organization's social justice campaigns. Some of those campaigns were related to my journalism in Colombia, as ARSN worked in solidarity with marginalized communities in that country.

Beginning in 2012, I started to lose my desire to participate in those activities. I resigned as director of the Centre for International Studies. I stopped attending ARSN gatherings. I engaged less and less with students outside of the classroom. I began ignoring interview requests from media around the world. I no longer saw any point to the journalism work I was still doing from home, and the frequency of my writing slowly diminished. I was growing increasingly cynical about the human condition and society in general. I couldn't understand why I was rapidly losing my motivation to engage in activities that I had been passionately involved in for years. I had lost my belief that the world could change for the better. Even worse, I was losing hope that it would, and I no longer cared. My responses to virtually everything became increasingly negative and cynical, leading my brother-in-law Rick to begin calling me "Garry Gray Cloud."

I would be overcome by negative thoughts in many situations. This was particularly evident whenever I travelled by plane or when Terry and the boys were away from me. When flying, I found myself constantly thinking that the plane was going to crash. I had the same thoughts when Terry was flying somewhere by herself. But it was more than a fear of flying, which I'd never previously experienced, because whenever Terry and the boys drove somewhere without me I was convinced that they were all going to die in a car crash. Interestingly, I never had those thoughts when I was driving, probably because I felt a degree of control when I was behind the wheel.

I also no longer wanted to spend time with friends and acquaintances. We had previously socialized regularly, either having people over to our house or going to their houses or out for dinner. But we rarely invited people over anymore, and I preferred that Terry socialize elsewhere. On the rare occasions that I did go out it would usually be alone to a bar to watch an English soccer game or to quietly read a book while downing a few pints. I used to be the life of the party; now I wanted nothing to do with the party. I was contracting, which meant I was shrinking my world down to a safe and manageable size by reducing the extent of the physical space that I existed in and the number of people that I engaged with.

My contraction also led me to respond bizarrely to other things. I had never had intimacy problems with Terry, but now there were times when I couldn't bear for her to touch me. It didn't relate solely to sexual intimacy, but any sort of physical contact. The two of us could be lying in bed and something as simple as Terry's leg touching mine would cause me to jerk my leg away. I couldn't explain what I was feeling inside; I just had this horrible feeling and an overwhelming need to not be touched. It had nothing to do with a lack of love for Terry, and at other times intimacy would not be a problem. However, it did leave Terry feeling rejected and confused, but I couldn't explain to her what was happening, because I didn't know myself.

Terry also had a habit of banging her hands down on the bed when she was talking. It wasn't really banging, it was more like letting her hand drop to the bed. It made a slight thud, but to me it felt like a bomb going off. I could barely focus on what she was saying because that banging just reverberated in my head. It instantly triggered me, and Terry couldn't understand why such a little thing would make me so irritable—and sometimes angry. Those hand movements were an unconscious act on Terry's part and therefore not easy for her to stop.

Communication had always been a strong point in our relationship, but we struggled to discuss all the things that were happening. We both began to think that the other person was being unreasonable. No matter how hard I tried, I could not control my responses, so I would simply claim that this was who I was now and Terry was going to have to accept that. For her part, Terry was frustrated because none of her communication and conflict mediation skills seemed to be working. Furthermore, my responses left her feeling like she couldn't do anything right.

Another common symptom of PTSD is chronic fatigue. The constant state of hyperarousal and hypervigilance, along with the related release of stress hormones, requires high levels of energy. Such a state is intended to be temporary; it is supposed to last just long enough to survive the threat and then things return to normal. But with PTSD, the hyperarousal and hypervigilance are constant, therefore exhausting. Of course, I had no idea what was causing the fatigue at the time, but I began to blame my short fuse on it.

There were many mornings when it would take great effort to get out of bed—and some days I wouldn't even bother getting up. The mornings that I did get up, I would feel lethargic throughout the day. I thought the fatigue and lethargy might be related to my bouts of insomnia, which were getting more frequent. Or perhaps I was just getting old. But I was only in my fifties and the changes seemed to be happening over too short a time—a couple of years rather than decades—for aging to be the culprit.

I thought that I might have some sort of physical ailment, so I went to the doctor. But blood tests and other physical exams didn't provide an answer. I went to a naturopath, but adjustments to my diet failed to have an impact. I then thought it could be allergies, but testing dispelled that theory. The allergy doctor did say that many people in Cape Breton have sinus problems that exhibit allergy-like symptoms due to environmental irritants. Believing this to be the problem, the only solution I could come up with was to leave Cape Breton. But this was not a particularly practical or desirable option because we liked living in Cape Breton and Terry loved her job as a professor at the university.

My behaviour began negatively affecting my relationship with Terry to the point that she started wondering how much longer she would be able to live with me. It caused a lot of anxiety for her. She never knew when she woke up each morning who she was going to encounter. Some days it would be the easy-going Garry of old. Other days it seemed that any simple act or conversation could trigger the emergence of an angry monster.

She began planning more and more work and social events in the evenings and weekends in order to get out of the house and away from me—no doubt in an effort to preserve her own sanity. As for me, I became alienated from myself. While my writing and teaching still reflected my belief that collective and compassionate action was necessary to achieve social change, I was personally becoming increasingly isolated, cynical and incapable of exhibiting compassion, especially towards myself.

I stared down at the faceless man. He was dressed in a bright orange tee-shirt and blue jeans. His hands were tied together at the wrists with a white plastic bag. His face had no recognizable features; no eyes, no nose, no mouth. It had been pummeled beyond recognition, caved in by repeated blows from a hammer, a rock or a rifle butt.

Beginning in 2013, I would feel extremely burned out during the second half of the school year. I initially put it down to the demands of homeschooling, but that didn't really make sense to me. After all, I had worked hard at many different and demanding jobs throughout my life, so why was I suddenly feeling so burned out by February each school year? Perhaps it was a matter of aging? But again, why had it happened so suddenly?

Our solution to my "burned out" state was for me to take a couple of weeks of rest and relaxation in Cuba at the end of every April and return rejuvenated for the final two months of homeschool. Terry was an ardent proponent of this solution because she was finding me intolerable by the time March arrived. I had previously only visited Cuba for work, including the launch of my book *Capitalism: A Structural Genocide*, which had taken place in Havana in May 2012. But from Canada it was easy and relatively inexpensive to book resort vacations to the Caribbean island. Not only had I never previously considered taking packaged vacations, I had even been critical of them. There was something disturbing about people from rich countries enjoying the pristine tropical beaches of poorer nations while being waited on hand and foot by locals.

I justified beginning to take such vacations in socialist Cuba because the government pocketed most of the revenues from resorts and used that money to fund the country's stellar social programs such as health care and education for the Cuban people. This contrasted sharply with resorts in capitalist Latin American nations, like Mexico and the Dominican Republic, where most of the money left those countries in the pockets of foreign hotel chains.

Every year I would stay in a different part of Cuba so that I could leave the resort and engage in some journalism work while there. This allowed me to gain insights into Cuban life in such diverse parts of the country as Havana, Santiago de Cuba, Holguin and Matanzas. Doing journalism in Cuba was very different to my work in Colombia. I felt little stress and anxiety compared to the intensity of Colombia's conflict zones, where I was on edge all the time.

On one such visit, in early May 2014, I travelled to Havana for a pre-arranged interview with one of the leaders of Colombia's largest guerrilla group, the Revolutionary Armed Forces of Colombia (FARC). Rebel negotiators were in Cuba at the time participating in peace talks with representatives of the Colombian government. Suddenly, only hours before I was scheduled to meet with the guerrillas, I emailed my FARC contact and cancelled the interview. I just didn't feel up to it. At the time I didn't understand my response; in fact, I found it truly disturbing that I would walk away from such a journalistic opportunity. It wasn't until after my breakdown more than two years later that I realized PTSD was the reason I couldn't handle engaging in any journalism that related to Colombia's armed conflict, even though the interview would have taken place in Cuba.

Interestingly, one year later I responded very differently when I visited Palestine. Terry and I had been invited to speak at Birzeit University in the West Bank. While there, we spent a week travelling around the West Bank from East Jerusalem to Bethlehem to Ramallah to Nablus to investigate the situation for Palestinians living under the Israeli military occupation. Neither Israeli military checkpoints nor the general insecurity of the region bothered me. In fact, I felt like my old self while there. Even though we visited the West Bank eighteen months before my breakdown, my PTSD symptoms were already making me dysfunctional at home. But my hyperarousal and hypervigilance were rational responses to the tensions in that part of the world. I was like a soldier with PTSD who felt more comfortable in a conflict zone than at home.

In June 2015, we moved into a small two-bedroom apartment in Havana for three months. Terry was in Cuba to conduct research, and I mostly hung out with Morgan and Owen while doing some journalism on the side. Our apartment was located in the Havana neighbourhood of Belén. It was a typical urban neighbourhood where Cubans went about their regular daily activities sans tourists. And while overall we enjoyed our stay in Cuba, Terry and I had very different perceptions of our time there.

Terry noticed that I was even more irritable and angry in Cuba than I had been at home. Later we realized that it resulted from my inability to deal with the changes in my daily life and routine. This was something new because I'd always been adaptable to a wide variety of environments, as my life trajectory illustrated. But now I felt an overwhelming need to be in control, and moving to a different country left me feeling vulnerable. But my PTSD symptoms were not rational responses in Cuba as they had been only months earlier in the West Bank because Cuba was not a conflict zone; it was a safe place. Consequently, my PTSD symptoms made me dysfunctional in Cuba just as they did at home.

Near the end of our Cuba stay, Terry and I had a revealing conversation. One of the foundations of our relationship had been our shared passion for social justice activism. But while Terry was still fully engaged in that work, I wasn't. She was developing a life separate from me. I couldn't help but feel that she viewed me as less of a person because of my growing abstention from activism. So I confessed to her that I didn't feel I was good enough for her anymore. For her part, Terry didn't feel that she could do anything right because of my consistently irritable and angry responses to her. Neither one of us felt that we were good enough for the other and this, despite our love for each other, led us for the first time to seriously question the viability of our relationship.

Upon returning home to Cape Breton, my condition continued to deteriorate. My irritability was getting worse and my angry outbursts were becoming ever more frequent. Furthermore, I had begun hurting myself. Sometimes when I got angry, I would punch myself in the face several times. It was a new level of anger and I didn't understand what was happening. I didn't know why I had this uncontrollable desire to hurt myself. Naturally, this new development was deeply troubling for Terry too.

I was also becoming more depressed and at times began wishing that I were dead. I hadn't yet contemplated committing suicide, but the thought of dying was somehow soothing; it would be an escape from the misery. The situation was beginning to get dire, but we still had no idea what was happening to me. Initially, the changes in my personality appeared so gradually that we'd barely noticed them. But by the fall of 2015 it had become evident that I was a very different person than I had been only three years earlier.

One afternoon that fall, while we were sitting on our deck discussing my health, Terry suggested that I might have PTSD because of my work in Colombia's war zones. I quickly dismissed the suggestion. Neither Terry nor I knew anything about PTSD. As far as I was concerned, it was an illness that affected soldiers in combat. I was not a soldier and I had not fought in combat. And while Terry was thinking about my experiences in Colombia's war zones, I pointed out that the last time I'd worked as a journalist in that country was three years earlier. Surely, if I had PTSD it would have occurred while I was working in Colombia or immediately afterwards, not several years later. Furthermore, there was no way that I could have a mental illness.

Nevertheless, Terry suggested that I see a therapist, but I remained stubbornly convinced that the problem was related to my physical health. After all, most of its manifestations appeared to be physical—chronic fatigue, headaches, nausea, diarrhea and sinus problems. Clearly, I was existing in a state of denial. And while Terry and I thought that things were bad at that point, my condition got a whole lot worse following my breakdown in that bar in Cali.

CHAPTER 4

THE EPISODES

MY BREAKDOWN IN THAT Cali bar consisted of an explosion of emotions related to past traumatic experiences, emotions that had been slowly seeping to the surface over the previous four years since I stopped working as a war correspondent. It was like a pressure valve had suddenly blown. The frequent crying that had begun on the day of my breakdown continued daily for the next few months, and often it would happen for no apparent reason. In actuality, the tears were the result of the sadness that had been triggered by subconscious thoughts of a past traumatic event. The tears would also be triggered by conscious thoughts or by certain topics of conversation, particularly political discussions, or by reading or watching the news. I began to avoid anything that might trigger a crying outburst.

In my weekly therapy sessions with Todd, I explained to him how I also felt intense anxiety throughout the day. And during the night too, when bad dreams and insomnia would frequently disrupt my sleep. He explained that the anxiety resulted from the constant anticipation that something bad was going to happen, which was a common and exhausting state endured by people with PTSD.

I was often overwhelmed by the thought of completing the simplest of tasks. I didn't feel I could cope with anything and didn't want to leave the house. On the rare occasions I did go out to run an errand, just driving to the store to pick up a couple of items would intensify my anxiety, and I would wonder when I got there whether I could get out of the car. I would skulk around the grocery store hoping not to run into anyone I knew because I didn't know if I could engage in a conversation without breaking down. I would be hypervigilant while walking up and down the aisles, looking for potential threats and also for people I knew. If I did see a familiar face I would immediately take evasive action. The aisles became terrain that I could utilize to my advantage because it was relatively easy to slip from one into another before I was recognized. But then I would have to stand in the checkout line terrified that I might suddenly burst into tears. Consequently, things I did effortlessly before my breakdown now required enormous mental effort in order to overcome the anxiety, and that effort was exhausting—and not always successful. Whoever said, "Don't sweat the small stuff … and it's all small stuff," clearly didn't have PTSD.

After a while, I changed my appearance so that no one would recognize me. For years my head had been shaved and I'd mostly worn black clothes, a carryover from my New York days. But now I grew back my hair and a full beard and began wearing different coloured clothes and a hat. People who knew me would walk right past me without a flicker of recognition—and that was fine with me. I didn't change my appearance only so that others wouldn't recognize me, but also so I wouldn't recognize myself. When I looked in the mirror I didn't want to see myself as I had looked before. It reminded me of who I had been and of all the things that I was no longer capable of doing. I wasn't that person anymore.

Socializing with other people was out of the question. Part of the problem is that PTSD can be a largely invisible illness. For me, and for many others with PTSD, most of the worst aspects of the illness occurred inside the home and were rarely witnessed by others. On those occasions that I ventured out of the house, I appeared outwardly to be my old self and people engaged with me as if that were the case. But on the inside, I felt broken, and the anxiety that emerged with the thought of having to interact with people in my "normal" way was overwhelming. Neither pretending to be normal nor spilling my guts about my PTSD every time I encountered someone was especially appealing, particularly when the latter would trigger uncomfortable emotional responses in me. Consequently, I would not engage with people at all on my bad days. And on the few occasions that I did engage when I was having a good day, it was difficult for people to understand my PTSD because I seemed so normal, despite the intense anxiety that was consuming me.

Because of the relentless anxiety, I stopped playing with my rock band The Misfit Boys. We had formed in 2009 and played two or three gigs a year and also recorded a few songs for compilation CDs. I loved performing live with the band, but following my breakdown I couldn't handle the anxiety that resulted from the thought of rehearsing, never mind playing in front of an audience. So the only music I played was at home alone. And it wasn't until after I was diagnosed with PTSD that I realized the degree to which my mental illness had influenced the music I'd recently been writing and playing at home. I had spent the summer prior to my breakdown recording a solo album in my makeshift home studio. The album was titled *What Tomorrow Will Bring* and it reflected my very dark and cynical view of the world.

PTSD also wrought havoc with my sex drive. On occasion, the adrenaline generated by my constant hyperarousal would kick my desire for sex into overdrive. For some reason, this usually occurred in the middle of the night when my insomnia would keep both Terry and me awake talking. My hypersexuality would result in us having intense sex two or three times in a few hours. But then, on other occasions, my contraction and chronic fatigue would prevent us from having sex for long periods of time.

Rachel Yehuda, Amy Lehrner and Talli Y. Rosenbaum, co-authors of a study titled "PTSD and Sexual Dysfunction in Men and Women," published in *The Journal of Sexual Medicine*, report: "Although it makes sense that a person—man or woman—who experienced sexual violence would have sexual dysfunction, trauma survivors with PTSD from other experiences also have sexual dysfunction. It does not seem to be the case that the problem stems from the type of trauma."

Sexual intimacy, or the lack thereof, can significantly impact a relationship. Part of the problem is that fear and sexual desire utilize the same neurological network, thereby causing emotional confusion in someone who has PTSD. "Individuals with PTSD may avoid intimacy because it raises feelings of emotional vulnerability, necessitates some degree of physical vulnerability, or is incompatible with constant hypervigilance," writes Yehuda and her co-authors. "For trauma survivors with PTSD, the relinquishing of control necessary to achieve orgasm may trigger feelings of helplessness, anger, and fear such that sexual activity becomes paired with negative affect."

I began spending about twenty hours a day in our bedroom. I turned it into a "man cave." I placed an armchair in the corner of the relatively small room where I sat surrounded by photos on the walls: photos of Terry and me together in Brazil, Spain and Colombia during happier times. We had cable TV installed so I could watch English soccer games at home instead of going out to the bar as I had done for years. In addition to soccer, I began binge-watching television series' such as *Mad Men*, *Masters of Sex* and *Velvet*. I had access to music and books in my cave. I would venture out into the living room for a few hours in the morning to teach homeschool and leave the house one afternoon a week to teach my class at the university. Otherwise, virtually every minute was spent in that safe haven.

Prior to the emergence of my PTSD symptoms in 2012 I had been a relatively social person. While there were times I enjoyed solitude, it was not something that I regularly sought out. Perhaps the most profound moment of solitude I'd experienced in my life was sitting on the bank of a river in the Amazon Rainforest one night staring up at the dazzling and awe-inspiring display of stars that were shining down on the darkness of the jungle surrounding me. But the solitude I craved because of PTSD was very different than that experience; it was rooted in fear and vulnerability, and it stemmed from a desperate need for security, not self-reflection. In short, I was a far cry from that twenty-nine-year-old adventurer who'd paddled a dugout canoe alone down a river in the Amazon Rainforest for ten days.

My thumbs were tied together behind my back and a blindfold placed over my eyes. The soldiers led me out of the cell and took me to a helicopter. The noise of the chopper was very loud and nerve-wracking. I was pulled up into the helicopter, to a large extent by my hair, and forced to lie amongst other live bodies. It was creepy lying on top of the bodies of people

I could not see and who I assumed to be in the same predicament as myself. The helicopter took off, and I had no idea
where we were going.

Despite spending so many hours every day in the safety of my man cave, I continued to have intrusive memories of disturbing events from my past. I'd had those memories for years, but I'd simply dismissed them as normal recollections. Previously, they hadn't triggered strong emotional responses. I guessed that those emotions were still repressed. But following my breakdown, those memories began to appear with greater frequency and increased intensity.

The intrusive memories were one of the most disturbing aspects of PTSD for me because they triggered powerful emotional responses. Numerous times a day, an image of a massacre victim, a woman being raped, a limbless landmine casualty or a combatant holding me captive at gunpoint would flash through my mind, leaving me feeling vulnerable and threatened. As Dr. van der Kolk points out in *The Body Keeps the Score*, "When people remember an ordinary event, they do not also relive the physical sensations, emotions, images, smells, or sounds associated with that event. In contrast, when people fully recall their traumas, they 'have' the experience: They are engulfed by the sensory or emotional elements of the past."

The intrusive memories distorted my reality in the moment in which they occurred. Whatever or whoever I was looking at would be infused with images from the past, disconnecting me from the present. They were very disturbing and made it difficult to concentrate on what was happening at that moment. The intrusive memories didn't only appear during the daytime; they also appeared at night. But unlike during the daytime, an image at night didn't just briefly flash in and out of my mind, it became embedded there. No matter how hard I tried I couldn't get it out of my head. I would wake up in the middle of the night crying with one of those images stuck in my mind. A pregnant stomach. A rape. A faceless corpse. A hacked-up body. A gun pointed at my head.

Initially, Terry would wake up worried about me. She'd try to comfort me, but to no avail. It happened so often that we eventually decided it didn't make sense for her to lose a night's sleep as well. So she would wake up and, upon hearing me sobbing, ask if I was okay. Then she'd go back to sleep. Sometimes I would turn on the television or read a book in an attempt to distract my mind, but that often led to an entire night of insomnia. Most nights I just lay in the dark crying until eventually the image went away and I'd fall asleep.

One night during such an episode, words describing the image of a massacre victim who was eight months pregnant came to me. It was much the same as when a new song would come to mind while messing around on the guitar. It just poured out of me, almost like a stream of consciousness. I scribbled down the words, which read like a poem.

Her hair black and matted,
Her face round and full,
Except for the hole in her right cheek,
A small round hole,
Surrounded by black and blue,
A neat and tidy hole.

A tee-shirt blue and mud splattered,
Stretched tight across her breasts,
Stretched even tighter across her belly,
"Eight months," said her friend,

A life not yet begun,
Now lost beneath that dirty shirt,
Lost to a hole in her cheek,
Surrounded by black and blue,
A death within a death,
A hole within a hole,
A neat and tidy hole.

I showed the poem to Terry when she woke up in the morning.

"Wow!" she said. "That's really disturbing." We sat there for a moment.

"Maybe you can compile a collection of poetry like this and turn it into a book," she said excitedly. Terry could see the possibility of a project in anything. I was the same, and I also briefly entertained the idea. It was so like us to take what we were going through and try to turn it into some sort of tangible outcome. We laughed at ourselves.

"It would depend on whether or not anymore of these poems come to me," I said. They didn't. I have not been creatively inspired poetically since that night.

The positive outcome of my PTSD diagnosis was that we finally understood what was happening to me. Before my diagnosis, my behaviour had appeared to be that of an irrational, selfish, inconsiderate jerk. But we now understood that my reptilian brain was triggering those behavioural responses before my rational brain could process what was happening. Knowing this didn't always make it easier for Terry and the boys to handle my responses, but at least they understood them. My diagnosis also helped Terry understand that my contraction from physical touching was not a rejection of her and that my irritability at things she did, such as dropping her hand on the bed, was not due to her inability to do anything right. Rather, it was my illness.

Nevertheless, while my rational mind knew I had an illness, it wasn't easy for me to accept. Throughout my life I had been strong-willed, determined and capable of doing pretty much anything I set my mind to. Life had always been a simple case of mind over matter for me. So why now couldn't I will myself to overcome the anxiety? To be more social again? To stop myself from getting angry? Why couldn't I make myself stop crying and breaking down? And why couldn't I stop those memories from haunting me?

"Why am I so weak?" I would ask myself. Not once, not twice, but over and over. I would verbalize it to Terry too. "I can't believe I'm so fuckin' weak!" I'd state angrily. "I hate myself!"

"It's the illness," Terry would respond.

While intellectually I knew she was right, that didn't stop me from beating myself up psychologically on a daily basis. I just needed to toughen up, right? But as Dr. van der Kolk noted earlier, the failure to control such "behaviors are not the result of moral failings or signs of lack of willpower or bad character—they are caused by actual changes in the brain." And this was the reason that, for the first time in my life, I felt I didn't have control over my emotional and physical responses. And this represented the most fundamental change between the old me and the new me. It also meant I had to come to terms with the fact that I had a mental illness.

Peering through the window of my cell, I saw a naked man who appeared to be in his twenties performing calisthenics in the dirt courtyard. Soldiers stood on both sides of him and every time he failed to perform up to their expectations, they beat him with sticks. Cheered on by their comrades, they whipped him until tears streamed down his face and blood down his back. Eventually the semi-conscious man was dragged from the courtyard back to his cell.

Most disturbingly, following my breakdown, I would frequently spiral down into a very dark place where I was over-whelmed by emotions, horrific images and suicidal thoughts. I would shut myself in the bedroom for the duration of those episodes, which usually lasted for several hours. Often, I wouldn't even be conscious of what had triggered an episode; they just seemed to happen for no reason. In those instances, the trigger was most likely a subconscious thought related to a past traumatic experience.

For months, those episodes occurred every few days, usu-ally in the evening. They often began with me crying, which was not unusual. But rather than the crying stopping after a while, I would begin to spiral and feel very depressed and despondent. Thoughts and images of past traumatic experi-ences would invade my mind. The images would not go away, and they were accompanied by a flood of emotions, including anger, sadness, guilt and self-hatred. Those episodes would quickly devolve into me sitting alone in the dark drinking rum and listening to music, usually something haunting like the songs of Nick Cave and the Bad Seeds. While I desperately wanted the episodes to stop, there was something inside that compelled me to continue spiraling down.

If Terry was around she would come in and sit with me and try to comfort me, but she soon realized that she couldn't stop the spiral. Like a force of nature, it would suck me down while she desperately tried to keep me afloat.

"It's going to be okay," she would say.

"No, it's not!" I would reply angrily through my tears.

In fact, the last thing I wanted to hear was that everything was going to be okay. It just made me feel more alone, like nobody understood what I was going through. At that moment it felt like the whole world was collapsing in on me, and I honestly didn't believe that what I was feeling would ever end. And later, even when I did realize that the episodes would eventually pass, I knew there would be another one just around the corner, either tomorrow or the next day.

"Make it go away," I would plead in desperation.

My words weren't actually directed at Terry; I would say the same thing when I was alone during an episode. But it made her feel helpless just the same. The spiraling would go on for several hours, slowly intensifying until it reached the point that I felt the only way to end it would be to kill myself. I'd envision cutting my wrists with a Stanley knife or getting into the car and driving head-on into a utility pole. Eventually, the thought of what my committing suicide would do to Morgan and Owen would lead me to dismiss that option.

But then I would begin punching myself in the face. I would punch myself so hard that there would be bruises and swelling afterwards. Terry would be frantic by this point. She would be in tears, at a loss for how to help. As the weeks and months passed she came to realize that, as horrific as those experiences were for both of us, they would eventually subside. But in the moment, it was agony for her too. And that only made me feel worse. And yet, I still couldn't stop it. Sometimes it would escalate even further, and I'd begin banging my head hard against the wall. Punching myself and banging my head against the wall were my ways of self-harming, but those actions were not intended to hurt me. Ironically, they were supposed to do the exact opposite: end the pain.

When I described my self-harming to Todd, he explained

that most people who self-harm are trying to gain control over the pain. Because the emotional pain was so intolerable and out of my control, I would deliberately hurt myself physically. I could control the physical pain in a way that I couldn't control the emotional turmoil taking place within me. *I* chose when the physical pain would begin, how severe it would be and, crucially, when it would end. Of course, I wasn't consciously aware of this when I first began self-harming. However, as the Canadian Mental Health Association points out, "People who self-injure are not trying to end their lives, but they can experience those thoughts. When they self-injure, they are trying to cope with difficult or overwhelming thoughts or feelings."

The self-harming would usually mark the beginning of the end of an episode. It actually did make me feel like I was regaining control. Either that or it was sheer fatigue that defused the situation. I would always feel terrible for what I had just put Terry through, which became yet another reason for me to hate myself. I also dreaded the fact that I would have to endure such an episode again the following day or the one after that. I was thoroughly convinced that I was going to have to spend the rest of my life enduring those horrific episodes, which is why suicide often seemed like the only viable solution.

Terry and I talked regularly with Morgan and Owen about my PTSD. They understood that it was a mental illness. They learned what had caused my PTSD, without hearing all the gory details of my work in Colombia. And they knew I was in therapy trying to get better. But while Owen was old enough to understand a lot of what was happening to me, Morgan, at only eight, felt far more vulnerable. My PTSD unsettled his world much more than it did his brother's.

We did our best to make the boys feel comfortable with my mental illness—to normalize it. Sometimes when I was triggered Morgan would ask me, "Is it your PTSD dad?" And when I'd sit crying in the armchair in my bedroom, they would often come in and sit on my lap and hug me. They knew why I was crying and they also knew it would pass. Thankfully, most of the bad spiraling episodes occurred after they'd gone to bed and they never saw me at my worst.

Nevertheless, there was no way to ensure that my PTSD didn't impact Morgan and Owen. And regardless of how much we talked about it as a family, the consequences for them of living with me and my PTSD would undoubtedly impact their development in various ways. For instance, because of my avoidance and contraction, I was engaging a lot less with Morgan and Owen outside the home. Terry would take them out to different places while I would remain in my man cave. We would explain to Morgan and Owen why I couldn't go with them, but that didn't necessarily stop it from affecting them psychologically. As the National Center for PTSD states, "Children may feel that their parent does not care about them when the reality is that the parent is avoiding places that are just too frightening." And in reference to the impacts of hyperarousal on children, the National Center explains, "Irritability and low frustration tolerance can make a parent seem hostile or distant, again making children question the parent's love for them."

Passing trauma on to the next generation can be a serious consequence of PTSD. Perhaps there is no more extreme and tragic example of this in Canada than the intergenerational consequences of residential schools. For more than a hundred years, encompassing virtually the entire twentieth century, some 150,000 Indigenous children were forcibly removed from their families and communities and placed into government-funded, church-run residential schools.

Many were subjected to physical abuse, forced to do manual

labour and even deprived of food in malnutrition experiments in addition to being prohibited from speaking their language or engaging with their culture in any other way. The objective was cultural genocide by eradicating the culture of Indigenous Peoples and then assimilating them into the dominant white settler society. One of the tragic outcomes was collective and intergenerational trauma. As one residential school survivor stated at a Truth and Reconciliation event in the Northwest Territories, "They took my culture, they took my language, they took me from my family, my people, the animals, my land, everything I knew and loved." He then went on to apologize to his three children for how he had treated them for much of their lives.

There are no reliable nationwide statistics for Indigenous Peoples regarding the prevalence of PTSD, sometimes referred to as residential school syndrome because of its unique cultural dimension. However, a 2009 report in the *Journal of Aboriginal Health* revealed that 64 percent of residential school survivors in British Columbia had the mental illness. In reference to intergenerational trauma among residential school survivors, Kevin Berube, director of Mental Health and Addictions at Sioux Lookout Meno Ya Win Health Centre, points out:

> Untreated trauma-related stress experienced by survivors is passed on to second and subsequent generations.... Direct survivors of these experiences often transmit the trauma to later generations when they don't recognize or have the opportunity to address their issues. Over the course of time these behaviours, often destructive, become normalized within the family and their community, leading to the next generation suffering the same problems. Many self-destructive behaviours can result from unresolved trauma. Depression, anxiety, family violence, suicidal and

homicidal thoughts and addictions are some of the behaviours our mental health therapists see when working with clients who have experienced direct or intergenerational trauma.

Cases of collective intergenerational trauma are also prevalent in war-torn countries like Colombia, where several generations have grown up amidst violence, and their traumas are likely to be passed on to the children who are born in the post-conflict era. Intergenerational trauma can also occur in individual cases of PTSD, and there wasn't a single day when I didn't worry about the negative effects my mental illness was having on Morgan and Owen. And that only further fueled my guilt and self-hatred.

In quieter moments, Terry would try to offer me encouragement by saying things like, "The same determination and perseverance that has allowed you to do everything you have done in your life will also get you through your PTSD." But I was rarely in a place to be positive. My response would usually be something along the lines of, "You need to flee! Get the hell away from me before I destroy you and the boys."

In fact, I regularly told Terry that she should leave me. I couldn't see why she would want to put up with me, to subject herself to those episodes. I was convinced that Terry would leave me at some point, so it may as well be sooner rather than later. I even toyed with the idea of making the decision for Terry by leaving her. At least that would get it over with, and it would give me a sense of control over the situation.

I also feared that I might end things by committing suicide, and I didn't want her finding my body. Studies have shown that people with PTSD are more likely to think about committing suicide or attempting it when compared to those with other anxiety or personality disorders. And it has also been shown that higher levels of intrusive memories increase the risk of suicide. Obviously, I didn't commit suicide. And, thankfully, Terry didn't leave me.

The dead man's lips were massively swollen, and his eyes bulged to the point that I couldn't help but wonder what was preventing them from popping out of their sockets. They were reminiscent of the exaggerated features of a ghoulish cartoon figure. Furthermore, the skin on his face, as well as that on his hands and arms, was sickly white and hanging loose as though it were two sizes too big for him. I surmised that the disfigurations resulted from a combination of the tropical heat and water. The cause of death wasn't immediately apparent, and the overbearing stench kept me from conducting a closer inspection of the decomposing corpse.

Those episodes, along with my irritability, anger, negativity and depression, made me feel like I was truly going crazy. The situation was compounded by my survivor guilt, which was rooted in privilege and the fact that I was still alive. After all, who was I to feel depressed when millions of Colombians had been killed, maimed, raped and forcibly displaced? I'd wonder how many of them suffered from PTSD.

I'd recall Macaria, who undoubtedly suffered from PTSD without even knowing the name of her mental illness. I'd sat in front of her small wooden house beside a jungle river in the town of Bellavista in western Colombia and listened as she recounted the tragic day when a homemade mortar launched by guerrillas crashed through the roof of the local church. Macaria and her daughter, along with most of the town's women and children, had taken refuge inside the church in an effort to escape the battle being waged outside. The stray projectile, loaded with shrapnel—metal, cement and nails—tore through the bodies of those inside.

"When we heard the blast, I threw myself onto the floor, covered my little girl and stayed there," explained Macaria. "When I tried to get up I felt that I was suffocating. I looked around and there was the smell of sulfur, something sickening."

Unable to walk because of shrapnel wounds to her legs and spine, Macaria lay on the ground staring at the ceiling and walls where various body parts were splayed. She recalls a long night of praying with the other wounded. But when dawn arrived, she explained, "Some of the children started to die. They were asking for help, but I couldn't help them." One hundred and nineteen women and children perished that day, almost 10 percent of the town's population.

Macaria's story was gut-wrenching, and even though a year had passed since the tragedy, the trauma remained—and she re-lived it every day. "There is something that is always there, it's like a ghost. There are moments that it goes away, but then there are moments when it comes back alive," she explained. "How should one feel when one wakes up from a nightmare to find three hundred and something pieces of body parts stuck all over the place? On the wall, on the ceiling, and on top of you." I didn't realize until long after I'd begun referring to my own demons as ghosts that I had probably subconsciously taken the term from Macaria.

Tragically, Macaria was far from alone among Colombians when it came to suffering terrible traumas and PTSD. More than five million Colombians had been forced to flee their homes by the violence and had to live the precarious lives of refugees. I remembered meeting a sixteen-year-old girl named Yamile who was living with one hundred and thirty fellow villagers in an old community centre in the city of Barrancabermeja in northern Colombia. They had been forced to flee their village after paramilitaries allied with the US-backed Colombian military arrived and massacred several residents.

I recalled sitting there talking to Yamile, thinking how much she looked like an average teenage girl from back home. But Yamile's biggest worries had nothing to do with boys or clothes or homework or any typical adolescent concerns. Instead, she described how she had to bear much of the responsibility for caring for her five younger siblings while her parents went out into the streets each day in a desperate search for food and other basic essentials for the family. Furthermore, Yamile's family and the other displaced villagers were being threatened again, this time by paramilitaries in the city.

"What are your hopes for the future?" I'd asked her.

"Peace, love and calm," she'd quietly replied.

I'd often wonder if Yamile ever found the peace, love and calm that she yearned for. Or was she still haunted by her ghosts?

When paramilitaries arrived in the remote Afro-Colombian community of Libertad in northern Colombia, they didn't forcibly displace the residents; they held them captive. One of their first acts was to organize a beauty pageant for local girls between fifteen and eighteen years of age. But this pageant was not just another example of a community engaging in one of Colombia's favourite pastimes, because the "prize" for the fifteen highest-ranking girls in the pageant was a two-week stay on the small farm the paramilitary fighters had commandeered for their living quarters. The mass rape that occurred during those two weeks signified the beginning of a brutal four-year occupation the residents of Libertad were forced to endure at the hands of the paramilitaries.

During those four years, most of the women and girls were raped by paramilitaries, and many of the younger children in the village were the result of those rapes. Furthermore, thirty-two men were executed during that time. A woman named Alejandra stood in her living room and described to me how the paramilitaries had murdered her husband in that very same room in front of her and her children. "They forced the door down," she said. "And they killed him right here inside my house." I couldn't help but think about how many of the people in that village must suffer from PTSD.

Only a small number of the millions of Colombians who likely suffer from PTSD have access to therapy or other forms of treatment. Colombian society, as is the case with most countries that experience war, is a traumatized society. And most of those suffering with mental illness don't enjoy the privileges that journalists like me from wealthy nations possess. They cannot simply decide to exit the war and travel to a safe country where they can receive treatment for their disorder. And this unjust reality only fueled my survivor guilt, which didn't help my situation, nor did it do anything for those millions of Colombians also enduring PTSD.

Survivor guilt and PTSD are the reality for many activists who work with marginalized populations in dangerous environments. Human rights accompaniers, refugee aid workers, natural disaster responders and other solidarity activists who work closely with traumatized people are at risk of becoming traumatized themselves. A study conducted by Meg Satterthwaite of the NYU Center for Human Rights and Global Justice revealed that 19 percent of human rights workers surveyed appeared to have PTSD. Satterthwaite notes that most of the human rights activists surveyed "reported that they were not prepared for the health effects of their work: 71%

said that they had received no or only minimal preparation for the emotional toll of human rights work, and 75% said their organization provided no or minimal support for dealing with such effects."

Activist Emily Apple, co-founder of Counselling for Social Change, which she formed after being diagnosed with PTSD, was also aware of this reality for many activists. "We'd seen so many people go through PTSD and realized that we are not making activism sustainable," she explains. "It is opening up that debate and saying that trauma work is actually part of the resistance."

Many activists often think they are just suffering from burnout and that they can simply push on through. After all, taking a break from activism often feels like you are abandoning people who are in worse straits than you. But ensuring good mental health is crucial in order to continue being an effective activist. As Apple notes, "I carried on far longer than I should have done and would have been far better if I had got help earlier, but it took me getting physically ill."

Similarly, I rarely thought about the consequences of my work for my own mental health, and to the degree I ever did, I believed I was too strong mentally to succumb to the psychological harm being experienced by the Colombians I was writing about. Such a view seems so incredibly naïve now.

CHAPTER 5

THE BUCKET

PRIOR TO MY DIAGNOSIS, I had known virtually nothing about PTSD, and I quickly came to realize that I was no different than most people: almost everyone has heard of PTSD but very few people actually know what it is and how it manifests. British TV personality Piers Morgan exemplified this in 2016 when he responded to Lady Gaga's revelation that she had PTSD due to being raped at nineteen by tweeting that the pop singer did not suffer from the mental illness because only "soldiers returning from battlefields do. Enough of this vain-glorious nonsense." He went on to state, "I come from a big military family. It angers me when celebrities start claiming 'PTSD' about everything to promote themselves."

Morgan's views not only reveal his ignorance about PTSD but also become a barrier to those seeking the care they desperately need. Why would a woman who has experienced a traumatic event like rape want to subject herself to verbal attacks such as those launched by Morgan against Lady Gaga? Morgan's response also highlights the lack of compassion in Western society with regards to not only PTSD but mental illness in general. The first assumption is that the person is trying to get away with something.

During the US Civil War, soldiers suffering from PTSD were routinely labelled as "malingerers," assumed to be trying to avoid fulfilling their military duty. Such views were not unique to that war. The 1970 movie *Patton*, which won the Academy Award for best picture, contained a scene in which General George S. Patton visited a field hospital during World War Two to pay homage to his wounded fighters. When he came across a soldier suffering from PTSD he slapped him across the face and insulted him. The scene was based on two real-life incidents that occurred in August 1943, when the famous general slapped a PTSD sufferer across the face with his gloves, dragged him out of the hospital ward and called him a "gutless bastard." A week later he slapped another soldier hospitalized with PTSD and called him a "goddamned coward." That same week, Patton issued the following directive to all officers under his command:

> It has come to my attention that a very small number of soldiers are going to the hospital on the pretext that they are nervously incapable of combat. Such men are cowards and bring discredit on the army and disgrace to their comrades, whom they heartlessly leave to endure the dangers of battle while they, themselves, use the hospital as a means of escape.

Thankfully, it is now widely acknowledged that PTSD is a serious mental disorder that can afflict soldiers who have experienced combat. But sadly, Morgan's view that it is only combat soldiers who can get PTSD is still a commonly held belief. However, not only was Morgan wrong in stating that a person cannot get PTSD from rape but, as mentioned earlier, studies show that women who were raped or sexually abused actually constitute the largest demographic in North America with the mental illness. And while the traumatic experience of a woman who was raped might be very different to that of a combat veteran, the symptoms of PTSD often manifest in strikingly similar ways in both cases.

Piers Morgan was not alone in the media in ascribing PTSD to war; much of the PTSD-related media coverage focuses on the military. A media study conducted by researchers at Drexel University showed that 63 percent of *New York Times* articles about PTSD published between 2005 and 2015 focused on military cases, when thirteen times as many civilians were affected by the disorder during that period. In fact, a greater percentage of survivors of sexual assault, non-sexual assault, natural disasters and car crashes get PTSD compared to combat veterans of the wars in Iraq and Afghanistan.

Almost one-third of the *Times'* articles portrayed flashbacks, nightmares and depression as the most common symptoms of PTSD, which is not the reality for most sufferers. Furthermore, movies and television shows often portray people with PTSD as violent. The stereotypical example being the "crazy" veteran who begins flashing back and, thinking he is back in a war zone, starts shooting everyone in sight. In actuality, according to the National Center for PTSD, only 9 percent of US adults with the mental illness engage in violent behaviour, although that number does increase to 19 percent among US veterans of the wars in Iraq and Afghanistan who have PTSD.

These sorts of media portrayals of PTSD help frame not only the views of the general public about the illness but also the views of those who unknowingly suffer from the disorder. As sexual abuse survivor Sarah Newman writes, "The portrayal of PTSD in the media definitely shaped my inability to see it in myself. ... I never considered that my anxiety and hyper-vigilance could be related to PTSD. I felt that the absence of flashbacks meant it couldn't be relevant.... those things just didn't seem as relevant as flashbacks. Isn't that what we see in movies?"

The media's focus on the military and war also creates a stigma for those who have PTSD from non-combat-related traumas. This was a likely consequence of Piers Morgan's response to Lady Gaga. As a result, those enduring non-combat-related PTSD often view their illness as lesser than that of soldiers. As Newman explains, "I still had trouble seeing myself as someone with PTSD. I began comparing my trauma to the trauma of others. I was imagining some hierarchy where I didn't have a right to be so traumatized. I mean, what could be more traumatic than seeing someone die? Those people need more help than me, right? That kind of thinking wasn't helpful."

> Gregorio's wife led me through a doorway into the only other room in the wooden shack. In the darkness I could make out a figure lying on one of the two double beds that almost filled the room. As we entered, the figure slowly rose up and with great effort slid down to the foot of the bed and into what little light shone through the door. I was horrified by the image I encountered. The man was dressed only in shorts and most of his face, chest, arms and legs were covered in raw-looking red sores, some of which were bleeding. Gregorio's left leg ended just below the knee. He'd stepped on a landmine.

It was the media's portrayal of PTSD that had me believing before my diagnosis that only soldiers could get the mental illness, so there was no way that I could have it. And while I later better understood PTSD, that understanding in and of itself didn't make it easier for me to get through each day. So

I continued my weekly sessions with Todd and we regularly discussed the challenges I faced functioning in daily life. He taught me mindfulness techniques to, as he put it, "lower the water level in my bucket." The water represented the emotions I was dealing with and when it reached the top of the bucket, just one tiny drop more would cause the water to overflow. In other words, when my capacity to cope with my trauma-related emotions had reached its limit, then the next issue I had to deal with, no matter how minor unto itself, would prove too much for me to handle. The result would be a disproportionate response to that final drop of a problem, through either anger or tears.

The mindfulness techniques were intended to help lower the water level by getting my mind to focus on the present and my body to relax, so that I could function without melting down so often. One of the most common mindfulness techniques used in treating PTSD is slow, deep breathing. According to Dr. van der Kolk, "Learning how to breathe calmly in a state of relative relaxation, even while accessing painful and horrifying memories, is an essential tool for recovery." Other techniques included doing exercises several times a day that involved tapping on acupuncture pressure points with my fingertips, primarily on the top of my head as well as above, beside and below my eyes. Todd also introduced me to lying down and listening to the sound of ocean waves through headphones for twenty minutes a day. The final technique was visualization, which required closing my eyes and visualizing a place in which I felt safe and relaxed. My place was a secluded tropical beach in Cuba. Todd also said it was important that I not overfill my plate. In other words, I needed to make sure that I didn't try to do too many things each day.

Previously, I would have rolled my eyes at engaging in

activities like deep breathing, tapping and visualization. I would have dismissed them as being "whoo whoo" stuff. But Todd convinced me that performing mindfulness exercises on a daily basis constituted a good "mental hygiene" practice. In the same way that we brush our teeth every day as part of our physical hygiene to prevent cavities, practising those mindfulness techniques daily would help reduce my anxiety levels and diminish the number of meltdowns.

In addition to the mindfulness techniques that Todd taught me, I also played the piano daily. I had begun teaching myself to play several months before my breakdown, and during my crisis I discovered that playing the piano kept my mind fully focused in the present, thereby stopping it from drifting into the past. Keeping my mind focused on the present also helped me not think about what lay ahead tomorrow or the next day or the next week. Thinking of the future—and convinced that bad things were going to happen and feeling like I had no control over them—generated huge anxiety for me. Consequently, I played piano for several hours a day.

I later learned that music and art are widely used in treating PTSD. In Canada, Jim Lowther, a veteran of the wars in Bosnia and Afghanistan, discovered that playing guitar helped him cope with his PTSD symptoms. "My guitar saved my life because the more I played the more all the noise in my head went away, it was life changing," he explained. "I still suffer with PTSD and always will but playing has helped me handle it better." In 2015, Lowther established Guitars for Vets, which accepts donated guitars and distributes them to veterans suffering from PTSD and other injuries. Meanwhile, in the United States, veterans have taken pieces of their old combat uniforms and other military paraphernalia and incorporated them into paintings and sculptures to help them process their trauma.

As the months passed, my mindfulness techniques did prove somewhat helpful. Nevertheless, there were still times when the bucket overflowed. Sometimes it didn't take much at all for me to feel overwhelmed. For instance, one afternoon I went out into the backyard to fix the boys' swing set. Within two minutes I'd become overwhelmed by the simple task and, unable to cope with my exploding emotions, threw the hammer across the lawn while yelling profanities at no one in particular. When I re-entered the house, I was already spiraling down.

My PTSD symptoms continued to dominate my life. In fact, for more than a year following my breakdown, PTSD alone defined who I was. If you'd asked me, "Who is Garry Leech?" I would've answered, "He is a person with PTSD." Nothing more. Not a father. Not a grandfather. Not a spouse. Not a son. Not a writer. Not a teacher. Not an activist. Just a broken man with a mental illness. I couldn't envision a life in which PTSD wouldn't dictate my every thought, feeling and action for every single minute of every single day.

In many ways this was true for Terry too. She couldn't imagine her life not being dominated by my PTSD. She began to wonder if living with someone with a mental illness meant being more of a caregiver than a partner. She also felt that our world had been effectively shattered and found it impossible to envision what our future might look like. In an effort to address her secondary trauma, Terry began seeing a therapist. She also joined a support group for people who had family members with a mental illness. Sharing experiences with others helped Terry to not feel so alone and to better cope with me. Terry also completed a training course that qualified her to provide education and support programs to mental health and addiction caregivers.

Even though I felt like a broken man, I still needed to function on a day-to-day basis. I still had to do homeschool with Morgan and Owen five days a week. And I had to teach my class at the university for two and a half hours every Tuesday afternoon. While I managed to fulfill my homeschool responsibilities, I wasn't as fully present as I had been during previous years. And with regard to my university teaching, that would always be the worst day of the week. I would often wake up on Tuesday mornings, usually after very little sleep, with a feeling of unbearable anxiety. Sometimes that feeling would lead to a meltdown and I would just lie in bed crying hysterically.

"I can't do this," I would say to Terry about teaching my class.

"That's okay," she'd reply. "We'll figure something out."

There were four weeks' worth of Tuesdays during the semester in which I was not able to function. Twice I called in sick and twice Terry taught my class for me. She also took care of homeschool on those days. Generally, it was far easier for me to teach homeschool than my university class because it took place in the house and I was comfortable being around Morgan and Owen. But teaching at the university required me leaving the house and entering a public place where I might run into someone I knew. And even if I didn't, I still had to stand in front of a class of twenty-six students for two and a half hours. Often, the thought of doing that was paralyzing.

Work is a major challenge for many people with PTSD. The symptoms of the illness, whether it's re-experiencing, anxiety, depression, difficulty concentrating or chronic fatigue, can interfere with job performance. Not surprisingly, people with PTSD tend to miss more days of work and have higher unemployment levels than the general population. The stigma attached to PTSD and mental illness in general makes it difficult for those afflicted to share with their bosses and co-workers that they have the disorder. As a result, poor job performance often creates the impression that they are lazy or have an attitude problem.

Thankfully, I didn't have to perform a demanding forty-hour-a-week job because there was no way that I could have done it successfully. However, I would've given anything to be able to. Before PTSD I was a workaholic. I'd spend twelve hours a day, six or seven days a week writing, researching, teaching, working in Colombia's conflict zones or engaging in social justice activism. But because of my PTSD, I could no longer do all those things. In fact, I would become anxiety-ridden and feel overwhelmed by the thought of doing just one of those activities. I constantly felt like I should've been able to more, but trying to do only a fraction of what I used to be able to do in a week would inevitably lead to a meltdown.

For the next twelve hours, I worked on one of the many human chains that wound their way over the mounds of rubble from where the firefighters were burrowing into the debris in search of survivors back to the perimeter of Ground Zero. We passed bucket after bucket of concrete chunks and other debris along the line to waiting dump trucks. In the other direction, we passed along items requested by firefighters, such as oxygen, water, power saws and body bags. We found no survivors. We also didn't find any bodies—only parts of bodies.

A classroom full of students wasn't the only place that made me feel incredibly uncomfortable. I felt that way in any crowded space. I could just about cope with going to grocery stores and places like that because they were relatively spacious, and I would be in and out in ten or twenty minutes. But sitting or standing still in a crowded space for any length of time generated massive anxiety and put me on the verge of a panic attack. Such was the case when I went out one evening with Terry and my longtime friend Stephen Paul.

Steve was an artist who lived in the south of France with his wife Mylene and son Oliver. I had known Steve since I was sixteen, when we met in Detroit shortly after my arrival in the United States. He was also a freshly transplanted British teenager, and he felt just as much an outsider as I did. We quickly forged a friendship that would survive for decades. In March, four months after my breakdown, Steve came to visit us to see how I was doing. It had been several years since I'd seen him. His long jet-black hair was fighting a losing battle to repel the encroaching streaks of gray, but his vibrant personality and sarcastic sense of humor remained fully intact.

It was St. Patrick's Day during Steve's visit, so he, Terry and I decided to go out to a local pub called Governor's to listen to some live music. I had not been out of the house socializing since my breakdown. Not surprisingly, I felt a lot of anxiety. Upon arriving, the three of us climbed the stairs to the second-floor pub. It was packed with people, and we had to wait for a table. We stood against a wall and talked while we waited.

Steve was not yet accustomed to being with someone with PTSD. Especially me. We had gone out to bars hundreds of times over the decades and were always very comfortable and lively in those settings. But in Governor's that night, I was full of anxiety and on edge. Most of what was said in the conversation the three of us were having didn't register with me. I was constantly scanning the room, checking out every face. And also on the lookout for an empty table.

"Hey, relax," Steve said, noticing my discomfort.

"I can't," I replied as I continued to fidget and look intently around.

"Hey, where are you?" Steve asked a couple of minutes later when I failed to respond to something in the conversation that had been directed at me.

"What? What did you say?" I replied nervously. It was taking everything in me not to fall apart, not to have a full-fledged meltdown.

"We can go home if you want?" Terry asked me.

I wanted nothing more at that moment than to flee out the door and race home as fast I could. But I didn't want to ruin the evening. I also felt that this was a test I had to pass regardless of how miserable it might make me. "No, it's okay," I replied. "I'll feel better when we get a table."

After about twenty minutes we did get a table. And, thankfully, it was along the side of the room, so I could sit with my back to the wall. That meant I didn't have to worry about what was behind me and only had to monitor the area in front. I did feel more relaxed once sitting down, but only slightly. Nevertheless, for the most part, I managed to enjoy the conversation as well as the lively, alcohol-fueled sing-a-longs of the Irish and Cape Breton folk songs that constituted the evening's entertainment.

Our evening out highlighted the elevated state of my arousal and vigilance. Being enclosed in a noisy room packed full of people caused my amygdala to identify the environment as a threat and to trigger my reptilian brain, which put me in survival mode. While externally I appeared to be listening to live music and conversing with Terry and Steve, inside my head my reptilian brain and my rational brain were waging a battle. The former was repeatedly telling me to flee because something bad was about to happen, while the latter was trying to reassure me that it was just a bar and there was no danger.

During the five days that Steve stayed with us I talked with him in detail about my PTSD. I'm sure it was strange for him to see his long-time friend suddenly break down crying on numerous occasions for no apparent reason. But it felt good to talk to someone other than Terry and Todd about what was happening. Steve came to understand the challenges I was facing and has been very supportive.

While it was good to see Steve, there was a negative consequence to his visit. The day after he left, I spiraled down for three days. It was the most prolonged episode I'd had, and it was laden with suicidal thoughts. The trigger was a conversation the three of us were engaged in at the dining table on his last day. Terry and Steve had always been overachievers, always full of vigour and passionate about the projects they took on in life. For Terry it was her social justice activism, and for Steve his artwork. I sat there and, as the conversation about those things progressed, my participation in it diminished. I ended up sitting there crying.

Over the next three days, during my prolonged episode, I explained to Terry what I was feeling during that conversation. I had sat there watching and listening to the two of them, vibrant and so full of life, while I felt broken. They were as they had always been, but I was no longer me. I felt like I didn't belong. I wasn't passionate about anything anymore. Nor was I excited about anything. I was simply trying to survive day-to-day, and there was no way that I could imagine ever being that sort of passionately engaged person again. In fact, I was convinced that I wouldn't be. Watching and listening to the two of them drove home the degree to which I felt broken.

Two other people that I talked to in detail about my PTSD were our friends Stephen Law and Evelyn Jones. They also lived in Nova Scotia with their daughters, Jade and Mady, albeit a five-hour drive away. Consequently, we usually only saw them two or three times a year. When they visited several months after my breakdown, I talked in great detail with them about what was going on with my PTSD. Steve and Ev had both previously worked in Colombia as human rights accompaniers, so they understood my experiences in that country better than most. And as occurred following Steve Paul's departure, I also had a meltdown the day after Steve and Ev left. Thankfully, it was only a one-day episode. Apparently, I could hold it together and endure the anxiety and stress of interacting with friends for a few days, but once they departed the emotions would come pouring out. My bucket would overflow.

> I repeatedly stumbled while trying to climb the stairs. I was blindfolded, and my hands were handcuffed behind my back. The soldier pushing me from behind was becoming impatient. I stumbled again, and he began beating me with what I assumed to be his rifle butt. Most of the blows struck me on the right hipbone, causing me to wince in pain and to curse at the soldier in English. While he probably didn't understand the words, he certainly recognized the tone, which only caused him to intensify the beating.

While there was only a small circle of people who I talked to intimately about my PTSD, thousands of others were aware of the gory details. Somehow, in February, three months after my breakdown, I had found it in me to write an article about my experience. It was motivated by the fact that my research revealed very little information about journalists with PTSD. There was a lot of material out there about military personnel with the illness, but not much about journalists, activists or victims of sexual abuse.

I was also inspired by the stories of others with PTSD. Following my breakdown, I couldn't bear to watch war movies, but I felt compelled to watch countless documentaries, such as *Poster Girl* and *Wartorn,* that told the stories of soldiers suffering from the mental illness. I also read all the books I could get my hands on, including journalist Mac McClelland's *Irritable Hearts: A PTSD Love Story*, which constituted one of the rare firsthand accounts of a journalist's experience with the illness. Even though those films and books triggered powerful and sometimes almost unbearable emotional responses in me, they also left me feeling affirmed and not quite so alone in the world. Misery does indeed love company. And so I wrote the story of my ordeal, which was published by *CounterPunch* and by *TruthDig*.

The response to my article surprised me. I was inundated with emails from people living with PTSD. Many of those emails moved me to tears as the writers shared their own stories and also because of the empathy and compassion they directed towards me. They were written by war veterans, journalists and survivors of sexual abuse. One war veteran wrote:

> After reading your article "The Ghosts Within: A Journalist's Struggle with PTSD," I was very saddened. My sympathies to you, sir, in every respect, for what you have gone through. I can relate. It generated a lot of emotion within me. I sat up and took notice.
>
> I, too, suffer from the plague of PTSD. I am a Vietnam veteran, having served in Vietnam with 5th Special Forces

in 1968–69. My exposure to this war and the horrible atrocities that I was part of have never ceased to this day. Although these experiences happened to me almost 50 years ago, the "ghosts" remain. I call them demons, but what the hell, sounds the same to me. They are all ugly and constantly rear their dark evil heads regularly, these days anyway.

I, too, have been in therapy. But, like you mentioned, and although the therapy is helpful, I am aware that I will never be the same because of what has happened … just recognize the triggers and learn to cope. … My wife and I go through lots of "coping" activities nowadays.

Another respondent stated:

I was very moved by your essay of your experience of PTSD. I too suffer from this, and my life has been seriously compromised by its effects. Although the origins of the trauma are different, your description of how it manifested is similar to my personal experience.

In addition to describing his own traumatic experiences and the consequences, one man wrote:

I want to thank you for sharing your journey with we readers at *CounterPunch*. I've always appreciated your work, and now, after your explanation, the trauma and pain connected with it, I have a much deeper appreciation for your sacrifice.… I share this because I cannot imagine how you have endured the heartbreaking pain of the work you have done for so long. It is not surprising that you experienced the emotional response you have; rather it is amazing you functioned for so long before your feelings finally became overwhelming. Know that those of us who have even a small experience of what you have endured have the deepest respect and empathy possible for you Garry.

And people who didn't suffer from PTSD also responded:

I just had the pleasure of reading your article about your PTSD experience on *CounterPunch*. It was an excellent read. Thank you for spilling your guts like that. Obviously countless people are able to relate and find some kind of comfort vis à-vis their own issue and it also just makes for a very compelling article. I browse *CounterPunch* daily but don't read every article. I kind of rolled my eyes as I started yours, you know, "Journalist whines about his PTSD," and for that, I apologize. What a serious issue that I have never taken the time to learn about. You have done some fantastic work which has served others and seem to have paid a price for it.

Another wrote:

I read your article and found myself wanting to comment. I am not a journalist, never put myself in the kind of danger you experienced and don't have PTSD. Nevertheless, I would like to suggest that your episode of crying was not a sign of disease, but of health. From the way you described it, it seems that you were suddenly weeping for the futility of all your efforts and the failure of your strength as the world continued to get ever more horrible. You were weeping for all the horrible inhumanity you saw, and, frankly, in a magnificent way. I think there are few people with that emotional capacity and you should not think of it as a disease, but as a sign of a large humanity and therefore of health.

Some responses to the article were short and concise:

Thank you so much for the relentless honesty of your PTSD article. May you find peace.

The responses to my article touched me deeply. There was only one response that dismissed PTSD as hogwash. All the others were full of compassion and empathy. And, in the midst of my darkness and the cynicism I felt towards the world, those responses were heartwarming. For a fleeting moment, I didn't feel so alone and isolated.

Terry was also moved by the responses. "There is a real need for people with PTSD to know that they are not alone," she said. "You should write a book about your PTSD." I laughed. It was so Terry to once again envision a major project. But I was not in a place at that time to even think about writing a book. While writing the article had been somewhat therapeutic, it had also triggered many of my PTSD symptoms. It would be almost a year before I could seriously contemplate writing a book.

The responses to my article also made me momentarily consider seeking out a PTSD support group, but I quickly dismissed the idea. Writing an article about my PTSD experience was one thing, talking to people about it face-to-face was a whole different ballgame. When I was writing about it I was sitting alone at a computer. Sure, thousands of people would read it, but I didn't know them. I didn't have to sit with them while they read it. Talking about my mental illness in public was a far scarier prospect. Just thinking about it raised the water level in my bucket.

CHAPTER 6

THE JUNGLE

MY THERAPY WITH TODD was beginning to pay dividends. After five months I began noticing that I was having more good days than previously. And the bad days often weren't as bad. The spontaneous crying had diminished significantly, and the spiraling episodes were occurring less frequently and tended to last only about an hour. I decided to start going out occasionally—not to socialize with other people but by myself or with Terry. The only place I would go was Governor's Pub, and then only in mid-afternoon when it was mostly empty and I knew there was little chance of running into someone I knew. When Terry wasn't with me, I would sit by myself and read a book while having a few beers. As the months passed, it got easier and easier to go there, and Governor's became the only place besides home where I felt relatively relaxed.

I was largely okay being with people I knew well and who knew about my PTSD. I could also manage the brief superficial conversations I'd engage in with strangers, as long as I didn't feel trapped in a crowded place. The most uncomfortable people to be around were those who knew I had PTSD, but I had not yet talked to them about it. I didn't feel comfortable engaging with people as though nothing had happened; it felt phony somehow. But neither did I want to endure the emotional stress of explaining my PTSD experience to people I had yet to discuss it with. I found it easiest to simply avoid them. But there was no avoiding engaging with people in June 2017, seven months after my breakdown.

We had long-ago booked flights for all of us to visit my daughter Johan and my two grandchildren, Kathleen and Dylan, in Panama. Our friends Stephen and Tracey Harris and their daughter, Olivia, were going with us. Terry and I had numerous discussions during the couple of months leading up to the trip about whether or not we should cancel it. But I really wanted to see my daughter and grandkids. So we decided to go ahead.

We had no idea how I would respond to being in crowded airports, on planes, engaging with other people for two weeks or being back in Latin America. I handled the two flights to Panama City surprisingly well. We then spent ten days at a jungle lodge in the mountains, which is where Johan, Kathleen and Dylan joined us. We chose the lodge for a couple of reasons: it was low-season for tourists, so it would be quiet for me, and the kids could experience the rainforest. The lodge was situated on a jungle-covered mountainside. It consisted of a main building containing numerous rooms and a patio lounge area in front that was open on three sides. The patio is where we ate and hung out most of the time. There were also a couple of hillside cabins and, down below, a two-room river cabin. The river cabin's rooms were rustic, each constructed with rough-hewn, unpainted planks of wood and containing a double-bed and a nightstand. That was where Terry, me and the boys stayed.

Everyone in our group knew about my PTSD. And they

knew that I would need downtime alone each day to do mental hygiene and to not overflow my bucket. So each day I would spend several hours either in our cabin by the river or in a hammock on the patio of the main lodge reading a book or listening to music through headphones. Most of the time, this arrangement worked, and things went relatively smoothly. But we hadn't fully thought through how being back in the jungle might affect me, particularly in a country so close to Colombia: the two countries being neighbours. And so, not surprisingly, several episodes did occur.

> The afternoon tropical heat caused both Eros and I to doze off in the car. I was sitting in the back, and Eros was in the passenger seat directly in front of me. I awoke as the car came to a halt and I tapped Eros on the shoulder to wake him. He opened his eyes just as the barrel of an AK-47 assault rifle came through the open window, pointing directly at his head.

In the early afternoon of our third day at the lodge, I felt a crying episode coming on, so I descended the long staircase to our riverside cabin. Once inside, the tears began to flow and I rapidly spiraled down. I sat on the wooden floor against the wall and began drinking rum. I couldn't stop the horrific images and emotions from crashing around inside my head. The jungle noises that surrounded the cabin only further reminded me of Colombia's war zones. For the next seven hours, I sat there, an emotional wreck, getting drunker and drunker. Terry came down from the main lodge to check on me a couple of times, and I told her I was fine. I just needed to be alone. After seven months, we had become accustomed to those episodes. Later, when she again returned to check on me, I was passed out on the bed.

A few days after that episode we were all taking a walk along a quiet country road that weaved its way through the rainforest. At one point I heard the faint and distinctive sound of a helicopter in the distance. We sighted it off to our left near the horizon. It was coming towards us and the sound grew louder and louder. The sound of it instantly transported me back to Colombia. Because many of Colombia's conflict zones were in remote jungle, often the only access in and out of those regions was by river or helicopter, and the latter were routinely used by the Colombian military.

As the helicopter approached I began to struggle with intrusive memories that suddenly started invading my mind. The sound of the helicopter's whirring and pulsating blades reverberated in my head. It flew over us and as it disappeared off into the distance, the sound slowly faded away. The kids were excited to see a helicopter fly so close overhead. The other adults were not fazed by the occurrence. Meanwhile, I was struggling to hold it together during our walk back to the lodge.

When I arrived back at the lodge all covered in sweat from the heat and humidity, I went for a swim in the river in front of our cabin. I was attempting to eradicate the intrusive memories triggered by the helicopter as much as I was trying to cleanse myself. Suddenly, sitting on the bank of that jungle river, I began flashing back to Colombia. I couldn't stop myself from looking upstream, convinced that a boat carrying guerrillas or paramilitaries was about to come around the bend. Flashbacks were relatively rare for me, my re-experiencing mostly consisted of intrusive memories. But in that moment, every fibre of my being felt that I was in Colombia. I was convinced of it. I struggled desperately to locate and connect with my rational mind.

"I'm in Panama," I told myself. "This is not Colombia. It's Panama!" But I didn't believe it. I was in Colombia and about to encounter an armed group on that jungle river. I just sat there, staring upstream, waiting for the boat full of armed fighters to appear. I felt paralyzed as panic rose inside me. "I'm in Panama," I desperately reiterated to myself. "This is Panama!"

Terry came down to the river and immediately recognized the state I was in. She could tell when I was flashing back by the look on my face. She sat down beside me and, looking into my eyes, tried to reassure me that we were in Panama and not Colombia. But it was to no avail because, as Dr. van der Kolk points out, "No matter how much insight and understanding we develop, the rational brain is basically impotent to talk the emotional brain out of its own reality."

Eventually, the flashback passed, and I began to calm down as I recognized my surroundings. But though the flashback had passed, the episode was not yet over. That night I had a nightmare. I was lying inside a helicopter that was plummeting towards the ground. There were dead bodies lying on either side of me. I recognized the bodies; they were massacre victims I had seen in Colombia. One was a young man who had a bullet hole in his forehead. The other was a pregnant woman who had a bullet hole in her cheek. The helicopter continued its rapid descent.

"Why hasn't it hit the ground yet?" I asked myself. "Surely we should have crashed by now." But we hadn't. And it just kept plummeting. The weight of the dead bodies was pressing against me. I felt trapped and was struggling to breathe. "Why haven't we crashed yet?"

I didn't understand it. There was no way we could fall for that amount of time without hitting the ground. It was taking an eternity. Suddenly, my body began shaking. I opened my eyes and saw an angel. But I wasn't in the dream anymore. The shaking of my body had been Terry waking me up. I looked around the room; it took a few moments to get my bearings.

"You were having a nightmare," Terry explained. "You were thrashing around the bed and yelling."

I looked at her and said, "When I opened my eyes I thought you were an angel." Before adding, "Then I realized it was just you." We laughed and lay there hugging each other. Slowly, I began to feel grounded again. It took me a long time to get back to sleep.

The time came for us to say farewell to Johan, Kathleen and Dylan. Despite the episodes that had occurred, I felt that the trip had gone relatively well. I was glad that we had gone to Panama and that I'd got to spend time with my daughter and grandkids as well as my sister Karyn, who had joined us for the final few days.

We departed from the lodge and headed back to Panama City. Karyn flew home to Los Angeles and we boarded a flight to Toronto, where we had to make a connection to Halifax. The Panama-Toronto flight went smoothly, but when we boarded the plane to Halifax things began to go awry. We were sitting near the back of the wide-bodied jet and it was very hot. In fact, it was stifling. The plane slowly filled up but, after all the passengers had boarded, it didn't move. The captain finally announced that there was a problem with the air conditioning system in the rear of the plane and that mechanics were working on it. So we just sat there getting hotter and hotter.

I began to feel anxious. Actually, I was already feeling anxious, because I always felt anxious. But I was beginning to feel more anxious. As my anxiety increased I also began to feel afraid. I felt trapped. I was stuck in that tin can surrounded by hundreds of people.

"It's okay," I whispered to myself. "Just take deep breaths and relax."

But everything inside me was convinced that it wasn't okay. My hyperarousal and hypervigilance were in overdrive. "I've got to get out of here," I began mumbling.

Terry tried to comfort me by telling me that we were safe. She also let the boys know that it was just my PTSD. But I couldn't be comforted. I was feeling increasingly anxiety-ridden. I felt like I was being held captive again, and I hated that feeling.

"Get me out of here," I began yelling, louder and louder. "I've got to get out of here!"

A flight attendant came down the aisle to see what the commotion was. Terry explained to her that I had PTSD and being stuck inside that hot plane was triggering me. The flight attendant asked if I wanted to move up to the front where the air conditioning was working. The woman escorted me along the aisle while Terry remained with Morgan and Owen. The cool air in the front of the plane offered momentary respite from my physical discomfort, but I still felt trapped. I continued to get worked up. "I need to get off this plane," I said to no one in particular. "Get me off this plane!"

The flight attendant escorted me out of the still-open cabin door onto the ramp. It didn't help. I looked out the small window in the door that led down to the tarmac and through which they had taken the gate-check items. I began pounding on the door with my fists while pressing my face against the window. "Get me out of here," I yelled. "Get me the fuck out of here!"

I was having a full-on panic attack. An airline employee came down the ramp from the gate, and the flight attendant suggested that he take me back into the terminal. He escorted me up the ramp back out into the gate area, and I immediately ran over to the huge floor-to-ceiling windows and pressed myself against them. The expanse of openness beyond those windows helped diminish the sensation of feeling trapped that was consuming me. I slowly began to calm down. A couple of minutes later, Terry arrived at my side. The flight attendant had told her what had happened and allowed her to exit the plane. For a fleeting moment upon seeing Terry I felt relief. But then, suddenly, I began shouting. "Where are the boys? Where are Morgan and Owen?"

"They're okay," Terry replied. "They're still on the plane. The flight attendant is taking care of them."

"Get them off the plane," I ordered. "You've got to get them off the plane now! It's not safe!"

"They're safe …" Terry began.

"No, they're not," I screamed, cutting her off. "Get them off there now!"

Terry went to get the boys off the plane, but at that moment passengers began appearing from the ramp. The airline was disembarking the entire plane. Morgan and Owen appeared with a flight attendant, and I felt a huge sense of relief as I hugged them. We all sat in front of the large window staring out at the vast sky and I slowly calmed down.

As it turned out, they couldn't fix the air conditioning on our plane and had to find another one. Given my condition, the airline gave us the option of staying overnight if we didn't want to take the re-scheduled flight. Terry and I discussed it, and I decided that I just wanted to get it over with and get home. I was feeling calmer when we boarded the new plane two hours later and, thankfully, everything went smoothly.

I realized afterwards that I had been fine on all the flights where everything went according to plan: we boarded the plane, it taxied out to the runway, it took off, it landed, it taxied to the gate and we disembarked. The one problem that I had occurred when we boarded the plane in Toronto and things didn't go as planned: we just sat there. My amygdala sensed danger and triggered my reptilian brain, which then put me in fight, flight or freeze mode. In that instance, I felt compelled to flee from that airplane.

In my first session with Todd following my return from Panama, I described my various episodes to him. Regarding the flashback on the river, he suggested that one way I could have responded would have been to tell myself that if no boat appeared in the next ten seconds then I was safe. And to keep doing that over and over until my brain registered that I actually was safe. Todd also emphasized the positive about the trip. "You did it," he said, smiling. "I had my reservations about you going, but you did it."

"Yes, I did. But there were some very scary moments," I replied.

"But you did it," Todd re-emphasized. "And that's what's important."

A voice called out from behind me. I turned and saw a uniformed fighter armed with an AK-47 walking towards me. Several more uniformed men also carrying AK-47s emerged from the trees and bushes that lined the otherwise-deserted road. The black and white armbands on their sleeves identified them as members of the largest and most violent paramilitary group in Colombia. My heart began to race as the six paramilitaries approached me.

After returning from Panama I headed into two months of summer with no homeschool or university teaching responsibilities. I spent much of that time in the armchair in my man cave. I did occasionally go out to Governor's Pub to down a few pints and read. I also went on walks in the forest behind our house with Terry and the boys. On sunny days I'd sometimes sit out on the deck and enjoy the ocean view. I even did yoga occasionally with our friend and neighbour Amber, with whom I also talked about my PTSD experience. Things began to feel more settled. I had little on my plate and spent a lot of time doing mental hygiene.

During this period, I wrote a song on the piano about my episodes. It was titled "Ghosts" and the lyrics described what it felt like when I began to spiral down:

Here it comes again
Another wave of pain
Crashing 'round inside my head
Making me wish I were dead
Things I don't want to see
Coming back to haunt me
Trapped in my own private war
I can't take it anymore.

So I scream and I shout
And I try to shut it out
As I down one more drink
So I don't have to think … or feel
Cause it's all too real.

I try so hard to hide
From these ghosts lurkin' inside
I'm not the man I used to be
I'm just a memory.

While I still felt anxiety all the time, it was at its lowest level since my breakdown. My spiraling episodes were occurring only once every couple of weeks instead of every couple of days. And when they were triggered, they only lasted for about an hour. I was actually beginning to enjoy life a little bit. I wasn't doom and gloom all the time. For the first time in nine months, PTSD didn't dominate my entire existence. There were even days when I would forget that I had PTSD for a couple of hours. The relative tranquility of our summer led Terry and me to begin thinking that we were over the worst of my mental illness and on the road to recovery. However, some major bumps in the road still lay ahead.

My anxiety levels quickly began to escalate once homeschool and my university teaching began again in September. As the weeks passed, my anxiety increased further as did my hyperarousal and hypervigilance, which meant my irritability and anger too. Meanwhile, my intrusive memories remained as persistent as ever. The pregnant corpse. A decomposing body. A bullet hole in the head. Being held captive at gunpoint. The rape of my cellmate. All those ghosts continued to haunt me. I was also spending twenty hours a day in my man cave, and I realized that the improvement I'd experienced during July and August had just been a blip. I was still a very broken man. Evidently, I could only feel somewhat okay so long as I was doing virtually nothing with my life.

In October, eleven months after my breakdown, I had my most severe episode yet. It was triggered by a disagreement over the phone on a Saturday morning. I hung up and immediately felt myself beginning to spiral. I picked up the phone again and called Terry, who was at the local farmers' market with a friend. "I need you to come home."

"Are the boys all right?" she immediately asked.

"Yes. I just need you here now," I tearfully explained.

"I'll be right there," she said and hung up.

I sat in the armchair in my man cave as the avalanche of images and emotions poured over me. Morgan and Owen were playing in another room and were unaware of what was happening. When Terry arrived home twenty minutes later I was already in a deep spiral. She sat with me and, having learned her lesson months ago, did not tell me that everything was going to be okay. I just kept spiraling as the waves of emotion flowed over me. I was angry. Then I was sad. Then I was guilt-ridden. Then suicidal. And then I began self-harming. But this time the self-harming didn't subside. It went on and on and at one point I picked up a five-pound barbell and hit myself in the side of the head with it, causing my ear to bleed.

Terry fought to get the barbell away from me and after successfully doing so, she tried her best to stop me from punching myself and banging my head against the wall. At five feet eight inches, Terry is a relatively tall and physically strong woman who was partly successful in her efforts. But only partly. She could not stop me from hurting myself, only hinder me. Terry left the room and told the boys to go next door to Wayne and Barb's house and to stay there until we came for them. Morgan and Owen were unaware of exactly what was going on in our bedroom, but they knew something was up. Terry explained that Dad was having a really bad time with his PTSD.

Realizing that I was not going to stop hurting myself, Terry called 911. Within fifteen minutes a police car pulled up and two officers entered our house and then our bedroom. I was pacing back and forth when they arrived, and they convinced me to sit down in the armchair. I sat there crying while Terry explained to them that I had PTSD and what was happening. She was interrupted when the woman officer had to restrain me from punching myself. The officer grabbed hold of my wrists, but I then began hurling my head backwards against the wall. The other officer restrained my head.

Shortly after the police had arrived, an ambulance pulled into our driveway and two paramedics entered the bedroom. The police officers continued to restrain me while a paramedic, after obtaining my permission, injected a sedative up one of my nostrils. Shortly afterwards, they took me out of the house and put me into the ambulance. Terry, along with a paramedic and a police officer, sat in the back of the ambulance with me.

As I lay there staring at the back doors of the ambulance, I began flashing back. I was no longer in an ambulance in Cape Breton. I was in the covered rear of a pick-up truck in southern Colombia. I was being taken by paramilitaries to their camp. The police officer in the ambulance suddenly became the paramilitary fighter in the back of the pick-up truck, and I was staring at the back doors of the ambulance wondering how I could escape. Thankfully, I didn't respond physically—perhaps because the sedative had taken effect, but more likely because I was strapped down.

After we arrived at the hospital, I was lying on a gurney in a hallway in the emergency room for what felt like hours with Terry at my side. A police officer and the two paramedics remained with us in case I began self-harming again. And I did. I started banging my head against the wall and pleading with them to make the turmoil in my mind stop. Again, the police officer restrained me, and one of the paramedics injected me with another dose of sedative. The older paramedic attempted to engage me in friendly conversation, noting how difficult my journalism work must have been. But I just found his voice irritating.

Eventually, I calmed down, and Terry and I were left alone to wait for the doctor. The doctor examined me for head injuries and diagnosed me with mild concussion in addition to the cut on my ear and numerous bumps and bruises. Several hours later, I underwent psychiatric testing and we explained our PTSD story and my ongoing therapy and mental hygiene practice to the psychiatrist. He told us that we were doing everything right. Afterwards, Terry morbidly joked, "I'd hate to see the condition of those who were doing things wrong."

The psychiatrist suggested some possible medications that I could take. I was opposed to medication—and had been since my PTSD diagnosis. I was determined to get through this ordeal without drugs. But I wasn't being completely honest with myself because I had been self-medicating with alcohol since my breakdown. Previously I had largely been a social drinker, imbibing when I went out or when we had people over. But following my breakdown, my drinking increased steadily until I was hitting the bottle every evening. I usually didn't get intoxicated, unless I was having an episode, but several glasses of rum each night helped to ease my anxiety.

It is not unusual for people with PTSD to self-medicate with either alcohol or mood-enhancing drugs. In fact, according to the US Department of Veterans Affairs, "Nearly three-quarters of those surviving violent or abusive trauma report alcohol use disorders." Substance abuse is related to the chemical changes that occur in the brain of someone with PTSD. Therefore, not surprisingly, substance abuse is a common problem among the PTSD population. As the 24/7 helpline, AddictionCenter, explains, "Following a traumatic experience, the brain produces fewer endorphins, one of the chemicals that help us feel happy. People with PTSD may turn to alcohol and other mood-enhancing drugs, which increase endorphin levels. Over time, they may come to rely on drugs to relieve all of their feelings of depression, anxiety and irritability."

Following my breakdown, Terry understood and tolerated my resistance to prescribed medication, but the severity of the episode that landed me in the hospital led her to insist I try it for a while. I acquiesced for her sake and began taking 15mg a day of Escitalopram, known by the brand name Lexapro. Escitalopram is a selective serotonin reuptake inhibitor (SSRI) and is prescribed for depression. It is one of the five SSRIs that are commonly used to treat PTSD. SSRIs help regulate emotional responses by sending out neurotransmitters, such as serotonin, that carry a message to the parts of the brain that regulate mood.

A few weeks after beginning the medication, I did notice a difference in my mood. It wasn't shifting as dramatically from high to low. Generally, I felt more stable. The psychiatrist also prescribed an anti-anxiety medication, but I didn't like using it during the daytime because it made me too drowsy. I felt like a zombie and could barely function. It did, however, prove to be an effective sleeping pill at night when my insomnia was bad.

Despite that latest episode, more than nine months of weekly therapy with Todd had for the most part enabled me to manage my PTSD and cope with the symptoms. While this left me feeling better than I had during the peak of my crisis in the months immediately following my breakdown, I still had to contend with all the symptoms. But, thankfully, my meltdowns were less frequent and usually less intense. I still experienced intrusive memories, anxiety, hyperarousal, hypervigilance and contraction on a daily basis, but they were also less intense, thanks to my mental hygiene practice, the medication and not overloading my plate.

Todd had gotten me through the worst months of the crisis

triggered by my breakdown. He had brought me back from the edge. But while I was happy to be feeling a little better, my life was still largely restricted to me spending twenty hours a day in my man cave. Coping with my symptoms in order to simply exist wasn't enough for me. I wanted my life back; I wanted to begin living again.

CHAPTER 7

THE BREAKTHROUGH

WHAT COULD I DO to get my life back? That had become the most pressing question for me as we neared the end of 2017. I had become relatively stabilized thanks to my therapy with Todd, my mental hygiene and medication, but PTSD still dominated my life and, even more disturbing, it still defined me in my mind. I began to look in greater detail at treatment options. The most widely used form of therapy, and most successful in addressing PTSD, was cognitive behavioural therapy (CBT). According to the Anxiety and Depression Center of America, "CBT is a type of psychotherapy that has consistently been found to be the most effective treatment of PTSD both in the short term and the long term. CBT for PTSD is trauma-focused, meaning the trauma event(s) are the centre of the treatment. It focuses on identifying, understanding and changing thinking and behavior patterns."

There are various forms of therapy that fall under CBT. One of the most prominent is cognitive processing therapy, which helps people face their fears in a safe environment with the goal of changing their thinking and behavioural patterns. The therapy I had engaged in with Todd fell under this category.

There is also prolonged exposure therapy, in which the trauma survivor experiences prolonged exposure to the trauma memory in order to desensitize them to it. The form of therapy that I decided to engage in next was eye movement desensitization and reprocessing (EMDR). EMDR had become one of the more widely used and most effective treatments for PTSD and was approved by the American Psychiatric Association, the World Health Organization and the US Department of Veteran Affairs.

The first step in EMDR is to create a trauma history and determine which—if there are more than one—traumatic experience to work on first. The client then notes how physically distressing it feels to think about the particular trauma. Then the client focuses on certain thoughts and feelings related to the specific traumatic experience while the therapist holds up two fingers in the form of a peace sign and moves them back and forth. The client follows the fingers with their eyes while letting their mind go wherever it wants to go. Every couple of minutes the therapist stops moving their fingers and asks, "What's there now?" Then the process begins again. Eventually, the client reaches the point where thinking about that trauma no longer triggers physical distress, such as anxiety. Unlike conventional talk therapy, EMDR doesn't require clients to discuss their traumatic experiences in depth. While they have to re-experience them in their mind during the process, many people with PTSD find this easier than talking about their traumatic experiences.

The idea behind EMDR is that the client will eventually work through the trauma, desensitizing themselves to it and then reprocessing it. In other words, the amygdala stops registering the traumatic experiences as present dangers and the hippocampus files the memories away in their appropriate place. EMDR transforms traumatic experiences on an emotional and physical level and shifts the client's perspective of the event from a negative belief to a positive one. As the EMDR Institute notes, "For instance, a rape victim shifts from feeling horror and self-disgust to holding the firm belief that, 'I survived it and I am strong'." Importantly, the client gains insights, reaches conclusions and successfully reprocesses the traumatic experience through their own conscious and emotional processing rather than through a therapist's interpretations of their trauma. Once therapist and client have worked through the trauma history they then focus on present day triggers in the same manner to desensitize the client to them.

As Dr. van der Kolk points out, "EMDR loosens something up in the mind/brain that gives people rapid access to loosely associated memories and images from their past. This seems to help them put traumatic experience into a larger context or perspective." And as for the eyes following the moving fingers, it is not known why this seems to help. Some researchers have suggested it might trigger the same biological activity that occurs in rapid eye movement (REM) sleep, when the brain processes many emotional memories.

EMDR has proven most effective for those whose traumatic experiences occurred when they were adults rather than during childhood. Studies have shown that as many as 84 percent of single-trauma victims no longer had PTSD after only three ninety-minute sessions of EMDR. And one study revealed that 77 percent of combat veterans were free of PTSD after twelve sessions. Those results contrast sharply with the widely held belief that long-term talk therapy is required to overcome trauma. As the EMDR Institute points out:

> It is widely assumed that severe emotional pain requires a
> long time to heal. EMDR therapy shows that the mind can

in fact heal from psychological trauma much as the body recovers from physical trauma. When you cut your hand, your body works to close the wound. If a foreign object or repeated injury irritates the wound, it festers and causes pain. Once the block is removed, healing resumes. EMDR therapy demonstrates that a similar sequence of events occurs with mental processes. The brain's information processing system naturally moves toward mental health. If the system is blocked or imbalanced by the impact of a disturbing event, the emotional wound festers and can cause intense suffering. Once the block is removed, healing resumes.

Todd was not certified in EMDR, so I began looking elsewhere for treatment. Some of the cost of seeing Todd had been covered by the Employee and Family Assistance Program (EFAP), through Terry's job at the university. But I could only find two therapists in Cape Breton who were certified to do EMDR and neither one was on EFAP. In addition, our private Blue Cross health insurance did not cover any mental health therapy. I looked into the public health-care system but learned that it would likely take close to a year for me to begin EMDR through provincial medical services.

Terry and I decided not to wait, that we would pay out of pocket. And so I chose one of the two EMDR therapists in Cape Breton in order to begin the next phase of my treatment. This further illustrates the privilege that I enjoyed. For many people, particularly those from marginalized communities in Canada and the United States, the failings of the health-care system mean that they are often left in limbo with their mental illness for up to a year before they can receive treatment—and many of them don't survive the wait. According to the Canadian Mental Health Association (CMHA), "For someone struggling with a mental health problem, the inner battle that transpires during that waiting period can be overwhelming." Furthermore, the CMHA points out that more than one-third of those who are eventually seen receive inadequate treatment. And long waits are particularly dangerous for those who regularly have suicidal thoughts.

Long wait times, inadequate treatment and suicide are not only problems for civilians but also for military personnel who suffer from PTSD and other mental illnesses. Members of the Canadian Armed Forces are 50 percent more likely to commit suicide than civilians of the same gender and age. Tragically, between 2014 and 2016, at least 54 active members of the Canadian military killed themselves—a number that doesn't include veteran suicides. Retired lieutenant-general Roméo Dallaire, who has PTSD as a result of serving with United Nations forces in Rwanda during that country's genocide, was referring to the high number of suicides in the Canadian military when he stated, "Unless we treat mental health with the same sense of urgency as we treat a dangling arm on someone who has just been shot at, we will continue to take the fatal casualties."

Similarly, US government statistics show that male combat veterans commit suicide at double the rate of civilian males. According to the US Department of Veteran Affairs, twenty-two veterans commit suicide every day—one every sixty-five minutes. Not coincidently, according to a study conducted by the RAND Center for Military Health Policy Research, more than half of military veterans suffering from PTSD are not receiving treatment due to a variety of reasons, including long waiting lists at VA medical centres. Evidently, the US and Canadian governments have no problem spending money to send young men and women to fight wars on the other side of the world but are unwilling to sufficiently fund the treatment these people desperately need when they return home broken.

> Photojournalist Jason Howe and I were halfway along the block when gunfire again erupted all around us. Once more we took cover against the walls of the buildings that lined the street. This time the shooting didn't let up. We decided to make our way to the military base, moving slowly and carefully while keeping as close to the buildings as possible. When we arrived, the commander told us that the guerrillas had launched a large-scale attack against the town.

My first EMDR therapy session with Emily Bushell took place almost one year to the day after my breakdown. Emily was a tall, blond-haired woman who emitted a very comforting upbeat and positive energy. Her office was located in a relatively modern building compared to Todd's. A desk dominated one side of the room and opposite it was a brown leather couch. I sat on the couch while Emily pulled up a chair and positioned herself in front of me.

Our first session focused on whether or not I was stable enough to do EMDR. It turned out that I would not have been able to do it in the months following my breakdown because revisiting traumatic experiences when I was in such a vulnerable state might have pushed me over the edge. But my work with Todd had stabilized me to the degree that I could begin EMDR with Emily.

Following that initial session, we decided to implement a modified version of an intensive EMDR program. It called for eighteen hours of EMDR over six weeks; two ninety-minute sessions a week, although I ended up doing many more sessions after I had completed the intensive program. During the initial two sessions we mapped out my trauma history and selected the traumatic experience that we would address first. The trauma we chose to work on was my first experience in a war zone. But it was not as a journalist, nor was it in Colombia. It occurred when I was backpacking through Central America almost a year after my discharge from the US Marines. I was twenty-one at the time and crossing the border from Honduras into El Salvador. The Salvadoran border guards found a book of poetry in my backpack that contained a photograph of the author Patti Smith holding a walkie-talkie. Unable to read English, they assumed it to be subversive literature and detained me.

I was held in a cell at the border overnight and then transported the following morning, along with a middle-aged Nicaraguan woman, to a military base where the two of us shared a cell. We were both blindfolded when the soldiers placed us into the cell that first night. I managed to remove my blindfold by rubbing my head against the stucco wall, but my thumbs remained tied together behind my back with a shoelace, as were the woman's.

The next morning, three soldiers brought us breakfast and, to my relief, were unconcerned with the fact that I was no longer blindfolded. Like most of the soldiers I saw during my eight-day detention, they were young men in their late teens. They removed the Nicaraguan woman's blindfold and both of our thumb ties before leaving us alone to eat. After finishing her breakfast, the woman made her way into the bathroom. The three soldiers returned while she was in there. Upon realizing where she was, they retied my thumbs and disappeared through the bathroom door. I sat there with my thumbs bound behind my back, feeling helpless while they raped that defenceless woman.

Emily asked me to describe the image that entered my mind and what I felt when I thought about that rape. The image I described was me looking down on myself sitting on the floor of the cell with my hands tied behind my back. The image also included me watching that woman being raped by the three soldiers in the bathroom. I described feeling anger, sadness and guilt. Emily then asked me to be conscious of those images and feelings and to follow her two fingers with my eyes as they moved back and forth in front of my face.

Those images and feelings were the starting point but, as Emily had instructed me, I wasn't to hold onto them, I was to let my mind wander wherever it wanted to go. After a couple of minutes Emily stopped moving her fingers and asked me to take a deep breath. "What's there now?" she asked.

"It's still the image of the soldiers raping that woman," I replied. "Which is strange because I didn't actually see the rape, I only heard it. But in my mind that memory has always been me watching that woman get raped. I have vivid images of that rape. So I guess my memory is a memory of what I was imagining at the time based on what I was hearing, not on what I was actually seeing."

"Okay, go with that," Emily said. She began moving her fingers back and forth again. We repeatedly stopped and started with her asking me after each stoppage, "What's there now?"

Eventually, as my mind worked its way through the various aspects of the traumatic event, I came to realize that I felt anger and guilt at not stopping the rape. More precisely, I felt that anger and guilt because I didn't even try to stop it. I felt like a coward. I should have at least tried to stop it.

"But what could you have done?" asked Emily. "You were tied up."

"I knew that calling out for help might result in other soldiers joining in the rape," I explained. "But I could have at least banged on the bathroom door with my feet or my body to try and get them to stop."

"And if you had succeeded might the soldiers then have turned on you?" she suggested.

"I guess," I replied. "But at least them beating me up would have stopped them from raping that woman."

"Could they have beaten you up and then returned to raping the woman?" she asked.

"I guess so," I mumbled.

"Then go with that." And she began moving her fingers back and forth.

Over the next two sessions, and after more than three hours of staring at Emily's fingers moving back and forth, I came to the realization that I probably could not have stopped that woman from being raped. I also shouldn't feel guilty for not even trying to stop it because, as Emily pointed out, my response was a form of freezing. And freezing is an involuntary response to a dangerous situation, along with fight and flight.

I not only froze in that cell, but I also became emotionally numb. I didn't recall having any emotional response to the rape, either at the time or during the years afterwards. I felt that something was horribly wrong with me. After all, how can a person witness something so horrific and not respond emotionally? For years I thought I was some sort of monster.

Emily explained that the numbness I experienced was me dissociating, which is a relatively common response during a traumatic experience when neither fight or flight are options. Dissociative disorder is the mental separation of a person from some aspect of their self. According to the International Society for the Study of Trauma and Dissociation, "Dissociation is a word that is used to describe the disconnection or lack of connection between things usually associated with each other.... For example, someone may think about an event that was tremendously upsetting yet have no feelings about it. Clinically, this is termed emotional numbing, one of the hallmarks of post-traumatic stress disorder."

This description of dissociation captured in a nutshell not only my response to the rape in El Salvador but also the emotional numbness I felt following the other acts of violence I witnessed and experienced during that detention. It also described and explained the milder degree of numbness I felt following my traumatic experiences in Colombia many years later. And it made sense of why suddenly, following my breakdown, I finally began getting emotionally upset when talking or thinking about my traumatic experiences: the emotional numbness had begun to dissipate after I decided I no longer wanted to work in Colombia's conflict zones.

But for years, on the rare occasions that I did describe my traumatic experiences to friends or during media interviews, I was able to refer to them without exhibiting any emotional response. It never felt right to me, but then I knew nothing about dissociation at the time. I also wrote about my traumatic experiences, especially in my memoir about my journalism work, *Beyond Bogotá: Diary of a Drug War Journalist in Colombia*. There was one line in the book that never rang true to me, and that was because I didn't write it. One of the editors of the book returned the manuscript to me with her corrections and suggestions, and following my emotionless description of the rape in El Salvador she wrote, "How did this make you feel? For example, did it make you feel sick to your stomach?"

I didn't know how to respond to the editor. I hadn't felt anything. Once again, I thought I must be some sort of self-absorbed monster. Obviously, I should have felt something, right? But I didn't have it in me to tell the editor that I hadn't felt anything. I was ashamed. So I simply added in her suggestion, "I felt sick to my stomach." They weren't my words, but they allowed me to save face, at least with the editor and the outside world. However, to this day, that sentence has haunted me. It is the one sentence in the entire book that was not the truth as I saw it.

> Six guerrillas stood guard over me on that hilltop. They alternated between interrogating me and leaving me alone in silence. But then, suddenly, out of the blue, one of the guerrillas stared me in the eyes and calmly stated, "You know, if you are not who you say you are ..." He finished the sentence by pointing two fingers to the side of his head and jerking them upwards to imitate the firing of a gun.

My EMDR therapy raised another issue from my past that had also caused me to feel a huge amount of guilt. It was the most difficult issue to discuss with Emily and the thing in my life that I was most ashamed of. It related to my daughter Johan. While I was based in Panama with the Marines I'd had a six-month relationship with a Panamanian woman named Diana. Just days before my Marine deployment to Panama ended, she'd told me that she was pregnant. I had broken up with her six weeks earlier, just before being sent to the brig for thirty-five days for insubordination. Upon my release from jail to be shipped back stateside, she dropped that bomb on me. And it felt like a bomb, because both me and my life were a mess at that moment.

I had no choice but to follow orders and leave Panama and, upon my arrival in the United States, be processed out of the

Marines. I didn't know what to do with the information that Diana had imparted to me. I told myself that someone else must be the father. Or that Diana was lying about being pregnant because she knew I was leaving Panama and wanted to go with me. I grasped at any justification that could absolve me of responsibility for the situation. I was twenty-one years old, homeless, penniless, jobless and completely irresponsible. There was no way I could be a father, right? And so, I did nothing. But how could I have done nothing? I could by callously taking advantage of my privileged position as a white male in a patriarchal society. I had also bought into the macho military culture and its imperialist and sexist privileges in a Third World country. These were not excuses because there was no excuse for what I did—or, more precisely, didn't do.

I explained all of this to Emily. I told her how I had known for almost thirty years that I *might* have a child in Panama. I had also told this to both Jacqui and Terry, even though I no longer expected to find out for sure whether I did or not. So when I received that initial email from my daughter Johan in December 2010 it was not a total surprise. What was a surprise was Johan telling me that I had known she'd existed since she was six months old. She said her mother Diana had met with me when I'd returned to Panama on a backpacking trip almost a year after leaving the Marines and had told me that I was a father. I had no recollection of the meeting or the conversation with Diana.

I found it difficult to believe that I would forget such a meeting or conversation, so I phoned my brother Don, who had been in Panama with me on that visit. He confirmed Johan's story that I had met with her mother. I was astounded. How could I have blocked out that memory for all those years? I'd even returned to Panama again in 1989 to find out if I was a father because I had no recollection of already discovering the answer to that question eight years earlier. I couldn't locate Diana on that trip because she'd moved away from Panama City and I had no way of tracking her down.

And so, Johan's email not only delivered priceless happiness to me regarding my having a daughter and grandchild, it also made me realize that I had abandoned her. I'd known for all those years that she existed! I was a deadbeat dad of international proportions. What kind of person blocks out the knowledge that he has a daughter for twenty-nine years? What kind of monster was I?

Following this discovery, I felt horribly guilty and swore to myself that I would do everything I could to be there for Johan from that point on. I emailed her regularly. I visited her every year. I sent her money every month to help with her rent and university tuition. Regardless, my guilt still left me hating myself for what I had done to her. It seemed unforgiveable. I was so ashamed of what I'd done, not only to Johan but to her mother too, that I only discussed it with Terry and a couple of my closest friends. It was my big secret. The largest skeleton in my closet. The tale that I told everyone else was the same as the one I wrote earlier in this book about Johan finding me through the Internet, which was only part of the story. In other words, it was a lie by omission.

When I revealed all of this to Emily, she told me that I might never learn why I'd blocked out the memory of meeting Diana and learning about Johan's existence, but one possible explanation was dissociative amnesia, which commonly occurs with PTSD. In dissociative amnesia, both stress and trauma can cause a person to separate themselves from a memory. The rape I witnessed in El Salvador occurred less than three weeks after I'd learned that I had a daughter. It's possible that I experienced dissociative amnesia because the overwhelming helplessness I felt while witnessing such a brutal act of sexual violence against a woman caused me to block out the memory of just learning that I had a six-month-old daughter. After all, how could I possibly be responsible for the safety of a vulnerable little baby girl in such a violent world? But while I didn't know for sure why I'd blocked out that memory, knowing that I did left me filled with guilt and self-hatred.

Because I kept returning to the theme of guilt and what a horrible person I thought I was, Emily asked me a seemingly simple yet profound question, "Is it guilt you feel or shame?" I thought about it for a moment and was stumped.

"Do you understand the difference between the two?" she asked.

Again, I thought about her question and to my surprise realized I only had a vague idea and didn't actually *know* the difference.

"Shame is when you think you are a bad person," she explained. "While guilt is what you feel when you do a bad thing."

I realized that the overriding feeling that had consumed me all those years was shame. "I guess I feel both," I told Emily. "I feel guilty for abandoning my daughter and shame because that makes me a bad person. I think I was subconsciously ashamed of myself during all the years that I'd blocked out knowing about my daughter's existence."

"Okay, go with that," she said, and the fingers began moving. A couple of minutes later she stopped and asked, "What's there now?"

"I don't think my experience in El Salvador was the only motivation for my working as a journalist," I explained. "I think my journalism work in Latin America might also have been a way of subconsciously making amends for abandoning my daughter."

"Go with that," Emily said.

My mind couldn't stop linking those two Latin American women: my daughter Johan and the Nicaraguan who was raped in that Salvadoran jail cell. They both seemed to be at the root of my hatred for myself. And I felt ashamed for what I didn't do for both of them.

"What's there now?"

"I can't stop thinking about how it is shame more than guilt that I have felt all these years for abandoning my daughter and for not trying to stop the rape in El Salvador," I explained. "What kind of monster abandons his daughter?"

"So, you think you're a bad person?"

"Yes, I guess I do," I answered.

"But would a bad person spend so much time since then risking his life over and over to help others?" Emily asked.

I paused for a moment before mumbling, "No, I guess not."

"Okay, go with that."

I have long known that the guilt I felt in the years following my imprisonment in El Salvador was a significant motivating factor in my decision to become a journalist who investigated US foreign policy in Latin America. It had tormented me that my privilege allowed me to go on living my life relatively comfortably following my release from that Salvadoran prison while my cellmates likely continued to suffer or even died. I'd buried my head in the sand when I returned home, and it wasn't until years later that I eventually learned more about the US role in supporting El Salvador's brutal military. But what I hadn't realized until doing EMDR was that my abandonment of Johan might also have been a subconscious motivating factor for becoming a journalist. By trying to help other Latin

Americans, perhaps I was attempting to alleviate the guilt and also, as I now realized, overcome the shame I felt for abandoning Johan in order to prove that I was not a bad person.

EMDR also helped me realize how the guilt and shame from my El Salvador experience played a major role in determining the particular brand of journalism that I would practise. There are many ways in which I could have written about social justice and human rights issues related to US policy in Latin America without placing my life at risk in war zones. The subconscious reason that I chose to become a war correspondent became evident during our next few sessions of EMDR.

While watching Emily's fingers and thinking about massacre victims and my detentions at the hands of guerrilla and paramilitary groups in Colombia, my mind kept making its way back to El Salvador. It suddenly became clear to me why my guilt and shame had led me to Colombia's conflict zones— and to many more traumatic experiences.

"What's there now," Emily asked upon stopping her fingers.

"I'm thinking about how my work in Colombia was my way of subconsciously replicating my El Salvador nightmare," I explained. "I felt the need to replicate that danger in Colombia's war zones so each time I got out of my predicament I could do something about it. I could write articles and try to create awareness among US Americans about the role of their government in Colombia's conflict. I could do for Colombians what I didn't do for Salvadorans after my release from prison in that country."

"And what kind of person would risk their life over and over to help others?" asked Emily.

"A stupid one," I answered flippantly.

She smiled and, undeterred, asked, "Would a bad person, a selfish person do that?"

"No, I guess not," I replied.

"Go with that."

And so I went with that and with many other thoughts and feelings as we slowly and methodically continued to work our way through my long list of traumatic experiences. Sometimes I could think about them without exhibiting much emotion; other times I would become teary-eyed and feel sad or angry or anxiety-ridden.

Towards the end of each trauma that we worked on, Emily told me to bring back the original image I'd had in my mind of that particular traumatic experience and asked how disturbing it was. We would stop revisiting each traumatic experience when we reached the point that I no longer found thinking about it to be disturbing. I would still feel sad about it, but I wouldn't feel physically upset by it. For example, I would no longer feel anxiety in my gut.

The work on each traumatic experience would finally end once I had formed a positive belief about it. In the case of the rape in El Salvador, my belief shifted from feeling guilt and shame to believing that freezing and emotional numbness are natural responses to a traumatic experience and that my long-term response to witnessing that rape had been to spend many years trying to help other people who were suffering in war. So instead of being a self-absorbed monster, I was actually a caring and compassionate person.

And with regard to abandoning Johan, I formed the positive belief that I could not undo what I had done, and no amount of guilt and shame was ever going to change that. But I had been there for her for the past seven years and would continue to be there for her in the future. Furthermore, I was a different person now, which was apparent in the fact that I was not replicating the mistake I'd made with Johan with

Morgan and Owen, because I was fully present in their lives. Ultimately, and perhaps most importantly, Johan had forgiven me, so it was time to forgive myself.

But while therapy had helped diminish the extreme levels of guilt and shame that I felt for abandoning Johan, it hadn't eliminated them entirely. They will probably remain with me at some level for the rest of my life. I'm sure there are plenty of people, particularly women, who feel that I deserve nothing less, and who can blame them? I certainly can't.

Three weeks into EMDR I noticed that I was having fewer intrusive memories and was sleeping better. After seven weeks, the intrusive memories had largely stopped. This didn't mean I no longer had memories of my traumatic experiences, just that they didn't regularly flash in and out of my mind for no apparent reason. They could still be triggered like any other memory if something reminded me of them. But my emotional responses were no longer as powerful and overwhelming; instead they were only mildly disturbing and largely consisted of sadness. It was an incredible feeling of relief to not have those horrific images regularly invading my mind throughout each day. I finally felt liberated from them. Furthermore, my daily levels of anxiety, hyperarousal and contraction had diminished.

Emily and I continued working our way though the traumatic experiences that remained on the list. I would follow Emily's fingers and let my mind wander wherever it wanted to go. Sometimes it wouldn't drift far from the original image of the particular traumatic experience we were working on; other times it would go off on tangents. Sometimes those tangents proved to be linked to the trauma we were working on; other times they would take me to traumatic experiences we hadn't worked on yet. In those cases, Emily would usually bring me back to the original image of the one we were working on. And there were times when my mind simply drifted completely off-topic. For instance, I would go from visualizing a massacre victim to thinking about what I needed to pick up from the grocery store after the session was finished. Or I'd think about how tired Emily's arm must get moving back and forth like that for ninety minutes.

After addressing the first couple of Colombia-related traumatic experiences, most of the remaining traumas were resolved relatively quickly; it felt like they were falling like dominoes. Emily and I figured that this was because they were all rooted in the same experience: my El Salvador detention and my subconscious need to replicate my Salvadoran experience in Colombia but with a different outcome. For years I had subconsciously thought that if I wasn't risking my life then I was not doing everything that I could to help Colombians who were being harmed by war. Friends along the way had suggested that I had some sort of death wish. Part of me thought that they might have a point, but deep down I didn't think so. I now knew it was a compulsion to re-write the ending of my El Salvador experience that drove me, not a death wish.

Once I understood this and realized that I wasn't a bad person, I no longer felt compelled to be a war correspondent in order to do good. If I decided to return to that work in the future it would be because I chose to do so, because I wanted to, not because I felt compelled by guilt and shame. I no longer felt the compulsion to risk my life in order to feel good about myself. Understanding all of this helped resolve most of the remaining traumas on the list relatively quickly because they all kept coming back to the same root issues; they were all interconnected.

There was, however, one fundamental difference between my El Salvador rape-related trauma and my Colombia experiences.

In El Salvador, I felt partly responsible for the rape of the Nicaraguan woman because I didn't try to stop it. In Colombia, while seeing bodies of massacre victims, being caught in combat or being held captive at gunpoint were traumatic, I wasn't responsible for them. I didn't feel that my actions, or lack thereof, had caused harm to others. In fact, it was quite the opposite with regard to being held captive in Colombia because I was the one being threatened with harm. The overwhelming response I had to being held captive in Colombia was that of helplessness, with a healthy dose of fear thrown in.

One of the remaining traumatic experiences on the list fell into this category. It was also one that didn't resolve as quickly as most of the others. I had been detained by guerrillas in a remote village in eastern Colombia. The guerrillas who initially detained me turned me over to three other rebels who had pulled up in a white SUV. I was ordered to get into the front passenger seat while one of the guerrillas sat in the driver's seat and the other two climbed in back.

We departed the town on a dirt road and headed into the jungle. A few minutes later, directly behind my head, I heard the distinctive sound of the slide on a semi-automatic pistol being pulled back to shift a round into the chamber. I froze. The only reason to cock a gun is in preparation for shooting it. I waited for the crack of a gunshot. Thankfully, it didn't come.

I'd often had to contemplate the possibility of being killed while working in Colombia's war zones, particularly when being held captive, but that incident was the only time that I felt death was imminent. I actually believed I might die in that moment.

"When you think of that experience what image comes to mind?" asked Emily.

"I see myself sitting in the front passenger seat of the SUV and I hear the sound of the slide of the gun shifting a bullet into the chamber," I replied.

"Go with that," she urged. My eyes followed Emily's fingers back and forth as I relived that experience in the suv. "What's there now?" she asked.

"It's the metallic sound of that slide cocking the gun," I explained. "That sound to me signifies imminent death."

"What do you feel when you think of that?"

"I feel fear and anxiety."

"Where do you feel them?"

"In my stomach," I explained. "And tension in my upper arms."

"Notice that feeling and go with it." Again, my eyes followed her fingers.

"What's there now?"

"They were never going to kill me in that suv," I said. "They were simply fucking with me, trying to scare me. Those bastards probably had a good laugh about it afterwards, like bullies in school do."

"Okay, go with that."

While following Emily's fingers I fully absorbed the reality that the guerrilla in the suv hadn't intended to kill me, that he was only trying to scare me. Now that may seem obvious because I'm alive today, but there is a difference in knowing something intellectually and feeling it in every fibre of one's being. And that is what EMDR did for me: it transformed how I *felt* about my traumatic experiences, not only what I *thought* about them.

I allowed myself to fully absorb the reality that I survived the experience in the suv and was still alive today living with my beautiful family. The physical expression of my fear and anxiety slowly dissipated. That traumatic experience was further proof to me that I did not have a death wish, because my greatest fear in that SUV had been the thought of never seeing Terry and three-month-old Owen again. Death was the last thing I desired.

As the EMDR session progressed I also realized that the loud metallic clicking sound of the slide on that gun was a major cause of my hyperarousal. Sudden noises were major triggers for me; they instantly put me on edge. The sound of someone pulling back the slide on a gun in a TV show or movie would always trigger a physical response in the pit of my stomach. Terry dropping a spoon in the kitchen would trigger the same response. But as with my other traumatic experiences, I came to realize that the threat was in the past, it no longer existed, and I was safe now. I had survived and if I was ever to be in that sort of life-threatening situation in a war zone again it would be by my own choice, not because I felt compelled by guilt and shame. After twenty sessions of EMDR over three months, I felt that I was finally exorcising the ghosts that had tormented me for years.

CHAPTER 8

THE FUTURE

WHILE I WAS DOING EMDR therapy, my oldest son, Owen, read my memoir *Beyond Bogotá: Diary of a Drug War Journalist in Colombia* to learn more about the experiences that had led to my PTSD. When he was about halfway through the book, he came to me and said, "It's strange reading a book about my dad. Back then you were like the Indiana Jones of Colombia, but now you're just a PTSD grump." I laughed. He was right.

Because my PTSD symptoms had dominated my personality and behaviour for much of the previous five years, Morgan and Owen had little recollection of me before my illness. Owen's comment made me realize just how much I wanted to recapture some of the personality traits I'd possessed back then. However, I no longer wanted to be that person again; after all, that person was on a path to mental illness.

Thankfully, as I neared the end of my EMDR therapy, my mental illness no longer controlled me to the degree it had over the previous few years. I was no longer merely existing, I finally felt like I was on the road to recovery and was beginning to live again. I still had crying sessions and moments when everything was doom and gloom, but they were not as frequent. And I still endured anxiety, hyperarousal and contraction on a daily basis, but they were less intense, and so I could function much better. Perhaps most importantly, I no longer felt entirely defined by my PTSD. But as Dr. Judith Herman explains in her book *Trauma and Recovery*, the final step in recovery from PTSD involves reconciling with oneself:

> The survivor no longer feels possessed by her traumatic past; she is in possession of herself. She has some understanding of the person she used to be and of the damage done to that person by the traumatic event. Her task now is to become the person she wants to be. In the process she draws upon those aspects of herself that she most values from the time before the trauma, from the experience of the trauma itself, and from the period of recovery. Integrating all of these elements, she creates a new self, both ideally and in actuality.

I'd begun the reconciliation process described by Dr. Herman during my EMDR therapy. During our sessions, Emily had noticed that I repeatedly referred to myself back in my twenties as a selfish and horrible person that I didn't like. So, during one session, she asked me to close my eyes and imagine my fifteen-year-old self, who had just moved from England to the United States, my twenty-one-year-old self, who'd abandoned his daughter and witnessed the rape in El Salvador, my forty-something self, who'd worked as a journalist in Colombia, and my present-day PTSD self, all sitting together in a safe place.

I envisioned my four selves seated on the deck of our house and described each self to Emily. The fifteen-year-old me felt vulnerable and self-conscious, having just moved to a strange country where he was teased about his funny accent and the way he dressed. The twenty-one-year-old me was a selfish monster. The forty-something journalist me was full of guilt and shame but was also compassionate. The present-day PTSD me just felt broken.

"How does the twenty-one-year-old you feel about the fifteen-year-old you?" asked Emily.

I followed her fingers as my mind began to see things through the eyes of that twenty-one-year-old me.

"What's there now?" Emily asked after stopping her fingers.

"He doesn't like the fifteen-year-old me," I replied. "He thinks he's weak and needs to toughen up."

"Go with that," she said.

As my eyes began following her fingers again, I realized that the twenty-one-year-old me was a selfish and emotionally detached person because it was his way of coping with the vulnerability he'd felt when he was fifteen. The twenty-one-year-old me was the toughened-up version of the fifteen-year-old me.

"How does the forty-something you feel about the twenty-one-year-old you?" Emily asked as she began moving her fingers again.

I was back on my deck looking at the twenty-one-year-old me through the eyes of the forty-something me.

"What's there now?"

"He doesn't think the twenty-one-year-old me is a nice person. He thinks he's a selfish monster," I explained. "But he also feels sorry for him. He knows the twenty-one-year-old me was just trying to protect the fifteen-year-old me. He understands that the twenty-one-year-old me only evolved into the person he was because of a compassionate desire to protect the fifteen-year-old me, which of course, was himself."

"Now how does the present-day PTSD you feel about the forty-something you?" Emily asked.

I followed her fingers as the present-day PTSD me looked back at the me prior to the emergence of my illness.

"What's there now?"

"I want to be that forty-something me again," I replied. "I liked that person. He was compassionate and caring. He could also work as a war correspondent. I loved doing that work but don't feel I can do it anymore. I hate feeling broken like this."

"Go with that," she said.

I eventually realized that each significant phase of my life was a response to a previous phase. In a way, each phase constituted a new traumatic experience that attempted to compensate for the previous one. I also began to understand that I was not defined by only one or a few experiences in my life, no matter how traumatic they might have been. Perhaps, most importantly, I realized that I was not defined by my PTSD because I was constantly evolving, and who I was would shift again—and again. I was no longer that vulnerable displaced fifteen-year-old. Nor was I that selfish twenty-one-year-old who abandoned his daughter and her mother and didn't try to stop the rape in El Salvador. I also wasn't that forty-something guilt-ridden war correspondent. And I wouldn't be the broken PTSD me forever.

That EMDR session represented a reconciliation between the various persons I have been at different points in my life. As a result, I began to feel that I was a more complete me and that the process of developing my new self had already begun. And while I'll never again be any of the people I was before my PTSD, some of the positive aspects of those people would be part of the new me. Consequently, I began believing that the new me would be a better person than any of the old me's. And while Todd had repeatedly told a skeptical me precisely this during our therapy sessions, I now truly believed it. And this, in and of itself, had been inconceivable only months earlier.

So, am I cured? There are two contrasting points of view regarding the possibility of curing PTSD: it can be cured and it can't be cured. When we think of someone being cured, we tend to think of all evidence of the illness being eliminated. Take a physical illness like a throat infection. Strep throat requires antibiotics to cure it. And when it is cured the person continues with life as before, with no trace of the illness remaining. But there are many forms of cancer for which we do not use the term cured. A partial remission in cancer means the tumor is still there but it has gotten smaller. The person might no longer require treatment, but the cancer is not gone; it is a "chronic" condition that must be monitored.

Many clinicians consider PTSD to be cured when the symptoms have been reduced to a certain point. In other words, the person's re-experiencing, hyperarousal, avoidance and negative feelings score below the threshold for PTSD. But many of those symptoms continue to exist; they are just less intense than during the peak of the person's PTSD crisis. In other words, unlike people cured from strep throat, many people with PTSD do not return to the same state of health they enjoyed previously, with no trace of the mental illness remaining. Consequently, a person with PTSD, like someone whose cancer is in partial remission, could be considered to have a chronic illness. The person will most likely have to monitor their levels and types of activity as well as endure some of the symptoms for the rest of their life.

Despite having a chronic mental illness, I now feel that I can live a meaningful life again. I still have anxiety, hyperarousal, hypervigilance and contraction; however, they all exist at a much lower level when compared to the height of my PTSD crisis in the months following my breakdown. I continue my daily mental hygiene, which also now includes working out in the gym six days a week. Exercising first thing in the morning helps reduce the level of anxiety that I feel when I wake up and puts my mind in a more positive place. I can put a lot more on my plate each day than previously, but my bucket will still overflow if I take on too much. There also remains the possibility of a past trauma being triggered again at some point in the future.

Todd told me during one of my last sessions with him that it is possible to eliminate the D from PTSD. "It is a 'disorder' when it prevents you from functioning," he explained. I have now reached the point where I can function relatively normally on a daily basis. I still experience many of the symptoms, but because I can now function at a higher level, I no longer have the disorder part of PTSD. I only have post-traumatic stress (PTS). I have PTS because my traumatic experiences happened, and they have hugely impacted who I am as a person and will continue to do so because they'll always be with me. But nowadays, the water level in my bucket is at a much more manageable level and doesn't overflow as often.

My therapy has also made me realize the degree to which my body and mind are connected. I now not only feel better mentally but physically too. The degree to which I physically feel tension and anxiety in my body has diminished. My headaches, fatigue, diarrhea and sinus problems have also largely vanished. This body/mind connection also explains why I'd believed for so many years that I had a physical ailment when all of those physical symptoms were actually related to my mental illness. The body does indeed keep the score.

Shortly after completing my EMDR therapy, I began to wean myself off the SSRI medication. I wanted to know how much of my improvement was due to EMDR and how much of it was the medication I'd been taking for the previous six months. Over the ensuing month I gradually reduced my dosage until I was completely off the drug. During my weaning process and for a couple of weeks afterwards I experienced several discontinuation, or withdrawal, symptoms. Initially, I experienced light-headedness, nausea and increased irritability, but those symptoms didn't last more than a couple of weeks.

The worst, and longest-lasting of the withdrawal symptoms, were what are sometimes called "brain zaps." The zaps felt like there was an electrical cable running through my brain that would suddenly buzz and vibrate. There is no consensus within the medical community regarding the cause of brain zaps, although one theory is that they are brief, localized seizures. The zaps were not painful, but they were incredibly annoying and distracting. They would appear in rapid-fire bursts, five or six consecutively, and then nothing for maybe half an hour before another series of zaps. They were relentless for several weeks but then gradually diminished in frequency over the next month.

By the second month after my withdrawal symptoms had passed I realized that PTSD is not very forgiving. The D was back on the end of my PTS. While I could still handle putting more on my plate than in the midst of my crisis period, it was less than I had been able to cope with during the previous few months. My anxiety, hyperarousal, hypervigilance and contraction all increased significantly, along with my irritability and anger. I felt as though I was relapsing. And I sank into depression, distraught that I had not overcome my mental illness.

Thankfully, there was no significant reappearance of the intrusive memories, suicidal thoughts and spiralling episodes after I stopped taking the medication. EMDR appeared to have largely eliminated those symptoms. Nevertheless, I quickly realized that I needed the medication to help reduce my anxiety, hyperarousal and hypervigilance and to not feel overwhelmed and depressed every day. Therapy had effectively addressed the most extreme and worst aspects of my PTSD, but not all of it.

I have learned that overcoming PTSD is not a linear process. Even while on medication I have periods of days or even weeks when my anxiety increases, my hyperarousal intensifies, and I feel more contracted and depressed. Correspondingly, I usually experience a re-emergence of physical symptoms, including fatigue, insomnia, upset stomach and diarrhea. Clearly, remnants of my ghosts remain. However, it is my hope that, with continued therapy, the day will come when those ghosts will be completely exorcised and I'll no longer need the medication. But until that day, the new me is clearly going to have to manage my chronic illness.

So, who is the new me? To be perfectly honest, I'm not completely sure at this point. It has now been two years since my breakdown, and more than five years since my PTSD symptoms began to drastically change my personality and behaviour. There are aspects of my old self that I would like to recapture—like the positive aspects of my personality and the zest for life I used to possess.

There are some aspects of the old me that are reappearing. Terry says I am generally much more upbeat now and that I regularly joke around like I used to do. I am also beginning to occasionally socialize with other people. And the degree to which my hyperarousal has diminished since doing EMDR and taking medication is impressive. Things that would have triggered angry outbursts a mere six months ago only mildly annoy me now. The cat meowing or banging the closet door while trying to get inside. The boys making sudden noises.

Terry dropping something in the kitchen. I still notice these sounds, and often my heart still skips a beat, but I no longer react angrily because my brain isn't registering them as an imminent threat to the degree it used to do. As a result, Terry and the boys no longer have to walk on eggshells around me because the psychological abuse I had previously directed at them is no longer an issue thanks to therapy and medication.

Also, as I mentioned earlier, my intrusive memories have largely stopped, as have the suicidal thoughts. While I realize that they might appear more frequently again at some point in the future, these past months have been the first time in more than a year and a half that I have been largely free of the overwhelming emotional responses triggered by those memories and thoughts.

Terry also says that she can now talk with me about more issues without triggering and overwhelming me. For example, one morning Terry brought up a logistical question related to her upcoming trip to India to teach a ten-day course at the Earth University. "What do you think about me going to Rishikesh to do some meditation for a few days after my India course?" Terry asked nervously while she was getting dressed.

"Fine," I replied. "It makes sense, since you'll be so close."

She looked at me and slowly shook her head from side to side. "I couldn't even have asked you that question six months ago without you becoming instantly overwhelmed," she pointed out. And smiling, added. "Now all you've got to do is keep it together until then, so I don't have to cancel my trip."

In addition to recognizing some of the old me returning, I can also see some characteristics of the new me coming to the fore. For instance, I am a more compassionate person. Before my PTSD, I would encounter students and other people who suffered from severe anxiety or depression. While I would feel for them, I still believed that overcoming their anxiety or depression was ultimately a case of mind over matter. They just needed to buckle down and focus in order to bulldoze their way through it. I couldn't understand why they couldn't do that. But now, I have an enormous amount of compassion for anyone who is living with anxiety and depression, especially if it is related to PTSD. These are things that cannot be overcome alone; it takes a village to cope with a mental illness.

PTSD has also put me in touch with my feelings to a degree I had never previously experienced. Throughout my life I had largely repressed many of my emotions, but now I have no problem expressing them. In fact, I often feel that I don't have a choice, because they are so close to the surface now. Consequently, I understand myself far better and feel like a more complete person. This has not only allowed me to feel more compassion and empathy for others but also to exhibit compassion towards myself.

The new me also feels far more vulnerable than the old me. I no longer feel mentally and physically invincible. Even though I am feeling better than at the height of my PTSD crisis in the months following my breakdown, I still don't feel that I can trust how I am going to respond to things that people say and do. I might respond appropriately, or my PTSD might be triggered and cause a disproportionate response. I could get angry. Or burst into tears. Or I might spiral down and have suicidal thoughts. Or self-harm. Or all of the above. Not being able to trust how I will respond to things has left me feeling vulnerable all the time. This feeling of vulnerability affects what I do and how I do it in order to protect myself and my family, because my episodes impact them too. On the positive side, this vulnerability has made me more sensitive to how my words and behaviours impact others.

I have also learned the value of downtime and relaxing. I used to be an overachiever and would be constantly on the go doing things. But being that ultra-busy person often prevented me from stopping and smelling the roses. Some of my most precious moments now are hanging out with my boys and the tranquility I experience when spending quiet time alone. My mindfulness and mental hygiene practice also help me to focus on the present moment. Not only does this reduce the possibility of my past triggering an episode or thoughts of the future generating anxiety, it slows life down and helps me to appreciate myself and everything I have. I now realize that the present moment is not something to race through to get to the next moment, it is something to savour.

Sixteen months after my breakdown and five years after my PTSD symptoms began to dominate my life, Terry and I decided to put the new me to the test by taking a five-day trip to New York to celebrate our fifteenth anniversary. To my delight, and Terry's too, I went through the first four days without being triggered in any significant way. Every time something happened that would previously have triggered me, but this time didn't, Terry and I looked at each other in disbelief.

Our flight from Toronto to New York was delayed and I didn't get upset. Terry discovered one morning that she'd lost her purse the night before and I didn't get irritable or angry. We were crammed shoulder-to-shoulder in a packed subway train during rush hour and my anxiety didn't go through the roof, instead remaining at its new lower and more manageable level. The same when we were in an extremely crowded bar one evening. The only time that I felt really on edge was the day we were leaving for the airport to fly home and my subway card didn't work. I became instantly irritated, but it was relatively mild and passed quickly.

Our journey home involved a flight from New York to Toronto, where we had to make a connection to Halifax. Shortly after boarding our Halifax flight, the pilot announced that we would be delayed temporarily because the fuel truck hadn't yet arrived. And so once again I found myself sitting in a hot plane on the tarmac of a Toronto airport. But unlike on the previous occasion, I didn't feel trapped or have a panic attack. In fact, I had the idea to write down some of the things that had happened during the trip that previously would have triggered me but this time didn't. Strangely, at that moment, I couldn't think of a single one. I turned to Terry.

"I can't remember any of the things that normally would have triggered me but didn't during this trip," I explained. "Can you?"

Terry thought a few moments before replying, "I can't remember any either."

"We pointed out so many of them to each other," I said. "I can't believe neither of us can remember any now."

"*That* would have triggered you," Terry stated.

"What would have?" I asked, a confused expression on my face.

"Neither one of us remembering what happened," she replied. And we both smiled, knowingly.

The final test of the new me was the writing of this book. I was curious to what degree writing about my PTSD experience would trigger my symptoms. To my delight, it rarely did. In fact, it proved to be very therapeutic. However, one big remaining question for me was whether or not I had truly come to terms with the guilt and shame I felt for abandoning my daughter. Initially, I wrote the book without including that part of the story. I told myself that it wasn't directly related to the traumatic experiences that had caused my PTSD. But I came to realize that it was important for my recovery from PTSD and for my mental health in general. So I decided to include it for the world to see—and to finally remove that skeleton from my closet.

I also feel that writing this book is the first step on a new activist trajectory: creating greater awareness about PTSD. It is a topic that is obviously very close to my heart and, like many mental illnesses, it is not often discussed or well-understood in our society. Because of the plight faced by veterans of the wars in Iraq and Afghanistan, many people are now familiar with the term PTSD. Nevertheless, it still largely remains an invisible illness that most people don't really understand. I am coming out of the other end of my PTSD experience with a rejuvenated interest in social justice issues. I am back to writing the occasional article about global political issues and have written this book to generate greater awareness and understanding about mental illness. I still struggle to believe that the world will change for the better, but I have at least regained the hope that it might.

There is no doubt that PTSD has transformed who I am as a person. It has been a nightmare that I wouldn't wish on anyone. And I'm well aware that I am not yet done with it—and may never be. It's also been a living hell for my family. And it has changed Terry, Morgan and Owen too. They also now have a much greater understanding of PTSD and what it's like to live with someone who has a mental illness. But we have survived what we hope is the worst of it, and we have come out stronger and closer as a family.

I am finally moving forward with my life after having so many years of it being dominated by my past. Much of my life has been impacted by traumatic experiences. And now I am journeying through the consequences of those traumatic experiences. There will undoubtedly be many more twists and turns along the way. Thankfully though, at this moment I no longer feel entirely defined by my PTSD. And as long as I manage my chronic illness, I can function relatively well most days with my PTSD only dominating my personality and behaviour sporadically. I am lucky. Far too many others with PTSD are not so fortunate. I hope that, one day, we will live in a society that can exhibit the compassion and provide the safe spaces and support required for everyone with this illness to be able to exorcise the ghosts that haunt them, so they can return to a full and more rewarding life.

COLOMBIA CONFLICT TIMELINE
[1962–2018]

1962:   A US Special Warfare team visits Colombia, and its report to the US Joint Chiefs of Staff recommends that Colombia selects "civilian and military personnel for clandestine training ... with a view toward development of a civil and military structure ... and as necessary execute paramilitary, sabotage and/or terrorist activities against known communist proponents. It should be backed by the United States."

1964:   The US-backed Colombian military bombs communist peasants in the rural community of Marquetalia, and the survivors respond by forming the Revolutionary Armed Forces of Colombia (FARC) to engage in armed struggle to overthrow the government. Urban intellectuals influenced by the Cuban Revolution form a second guerrilla group, the National Liberation Army (ELN).

1965:   A Colombian presidential decree allows for the formation of private paramilitary security forces.

1968:   Law 48 allows the Colombian Ministry of Defence to supply paramilitary groups with military-grade weapons.

1969:   Colombian military order EJC-3 calls for the armed
         forces to organize paramilitary groups known as
         "self-defence committees." These are defined as "mili-
         tary-type organizations made up of civilian personnel
         in the combat zone, which are trained and equipped
         to undertake operations against guerrilla groups that
         threaten an area or to operate in coordination with
         combat troops."

1972:   Disgruntled socialist members of the new ANAPO
         political party form the M-19 guerrilla group, claim-
         ing that the National Front government stole the
         recent election.

1980s: Cocaine traffickers become increasingly powerful
         and, along with large landowners and the Colombian
         military, form new right-wing paramilitary groups to
         combat the growing strength of the leftist guerrillas.

1985:   M-19 guerrillas take over the Palace of Justice,
         which houses Colombia's Supreme Court. The army
         kills more than a hundred people, including eleven
         Supreme Court justices, in its two-day offensive to
         retake the building.

1985:   The government reaches a cease-fire agreement with
         the FARC and engages in peace talks. The FARC, the
         Communist Party and other leftists form the Patriotic
         Union party in order to participate in elections.
         Paramilitaries intensify their dirty war against leftists
         and assassinate more than two thousand members
         of the Patriotic Union—including two presidential
         candidates and four elected congressional representa-
         tives—over the next five years.

1987:   Colombian government statistics reveal that right-
         wing paramilitary groups are responsible for more

civilian deaths than leftist guerrillas, a trend that would continue throughout the next two decades.

1989: The government issues Decree 1194, which makes paramilitary groups illegal. Nevertheless, the number of paramilitaries increases dramatically over the next decade, and the military continues to collude with them.

1989: The government negotiates a peace agreement with the M-19 guerrilla group, and its members demobilize under an amnesty.

1990: The military launches a surprise attack against the headquarters of the FARC, bringing an end to the five-year-old peace process.

1993: The killing of drug kingpin Pablo Escobar marks the downfall of the Medellín cocaine cartel.

1995: The capture of the leaders of the Cali cocaine cartel marks the downfall of that drug trafficking organization.

1997: Regional paramilitary groups form a national organization called the United Self-Defence Forces of Colombia (AUC) and intensify the dirty war in FARC-dominated southern Colombia. The AUC fills the void left by the downfall of the Medellín and Cali cartels and becomes the country's largest drug trafficking organization.

1998: Newly elected President Andrés Pastrana withdraws two thousand soldiers and police from five municipalities in southern Colombia and turns the zone over to the FARC as a safe-haven in which to conduct peace talks. There is no cease-fire agreement during the peace process, and the war continues to rage throughout the rest of the country.

1990s: Colombia leads the world in kidnappings, with the FARC the armed group carrying out the most abductions.

1999: There are more than 400 massacres during the year, with the majority perpetrated by the paramilitaries.

2000: US President Bill Clinton announces a new multi-billion-dollar anti-drug initiative called Plan Colombia, making Colombia the third-largest recipient of US military aid. The initiative calls for the creation of a 3,000-strong Colombian army battalion trained and armed by the United States to combat the growing military strength of the FARC. Plan Colombia also calls for an intensification of the aerial fumigations of illicit drug crops, particularly in regions of southern Colombia controlled by the FARC.

2002: The peace process ends when President Pastrana orders the military to invade the FARC-controlled safe-haven. Meanwhile, the Bush administration begins providing counter-terrorism aid to the Colombian military.

2002: The US-backed Colombian military becomes the country's leading human rights violator by increasing its direct involvement in the dirty war against civilians through extra-judicial executions, arbitrary arrests, forced displacements and disappearances.

2003: The AUC paramilitary organization and the government begin negotiations to establish the terms under which paramilitary fighters will demobilize.

2005: The enactment of the Justice and Peace Law provides the legal framework for the demobilization of the paramilitaries. Following the AUC's demobilization, dozens of new paramilitary groups emerge, many led by former mid-level AUC commanders.

2005: More than four million Colombians have been forcibly displaced by the conflict over the previous 25

years, with the military and paramilitaries the principal perpetrators.

2006: Colombia's attorney general's office uncovers evidence of extensive collusion between paramilitaries, government officials, military officers and multinational corporations in what becomes known as the "para-politics" scandal.

2007: US corporation Chiquita pleads guilty in US Federal Court to funding AUC paramilitaries to the tune of $1.7 million between 1997 and 2004.

2008: The "false positives" scandal reveals that the Colombian army had been taking young men from urban shantytowns to the countryside and then executing them, dressing their bodies in combat fatigues and passing them off as guerrillas killed in combat. More than 3,300 of these extra-judicial executions occurred between 2002 and 2008.

2012: The Colombian government and the FARC begin peace talks.

2016: The two sides sign a peace agreement.

2017: The FARC demobilizes, ending its part in a conflict in which more than a quarter of a million Colombians were killed.

2017: Coca cultivation, which provides the raw ingredient in cocaine, reaches record levels.

2018: The smaller ELN guerrilla group continues its insurgency against the government.

2018: The paramilitaries continue to be the country's primary cocaine producers and traffickers.